JUMP Math
Book 1 Part 2 of 2

Contents

jump math™

MULTIPLYING POTENTIAL.

JUMP Math
One Yonge Street, Suite 1014
Toronto, Ontario M5E 1E5
Canada
www.jumpmath.org

Writers: Dr. Sohrab Rahbar, Dr. Sindi Sabourin
Editors: Megan Burns, Liane Tsui, Natalie Francis, Lindsay Karpenko, Daniel Polowin,
          Susan Bindernagel, Jackie Dulson, Janice Dyer, Grace O'Connell, Jodi Rauch
Layout and Illustrations: Linh Lam, Fely Guinasao-Fernandes, Sawyer Paul
Cover Design: Blakeley Words+Pictures
Cover Photograph: © Subbotina Anna/Shutterstock

ISBN 978-1-928134-29-9

Third printing June 2019

Printed and bound in Canada

Welcome to JUMP Math

Entering the world of JUMP Math means believing that every child has the capacity to be fully numerate and to love math. Founder and mathematician John Mighton has used this premise to develop his innovative teaching method. The resulting resources isolate and describe concepts so clearly and incrementally that everyone can understand them.

JUMP Math is comprised of teacher's guides (which are the heart of our program), interactive whiteboard lessons, student assessment & practice books, evaluation materials, outreach programs, and teacher training. All of this is presented on the JUMP Math website: **www.jumpmath.org**.

Teacher's guides are available on the website for free use. Read the introduction to the teacher's guides before you begin using these resources. This will ensure that you understand both the philosophy and the methodology of JUMP Math. The assessment & practice books are designed for use by students, with adult guidance. Each student will have unique needs and it is important to provide the student with the appropriate support and encouragement as he or she works through the material.

Allow students to discover the concepts by themselves as much as possible. Mathematical discoveries can be made in small, incremental steps. The discovery of a new step is like untangling the parts of a puzzle. It is exciting and rewarding.

Students will need to answer the questions marked with a ▯ in a notebook. Grid paper notebooks should always be on hand for answering extra questions or when additional room for calculation is needed.

Contents

Unit 5: Measurement: Length

Unit 6: Geometry: 2-D Shapes

Unit 7: Number Sense: Counting to 100

Unit 8: Number Sense: Introduction to Adding and Subtracting

Unit 9: Number Sense: Number Words and Story Problems

PART 2

Unit 10: Number Sense: Introduction to Skip Counting

Unit 11: Number Sense: Money

Unit 12: Number Sense: Number Lines

Unit 13: Number Sense: Addition and Subtraction Strategies

Unit 14: Number Sense: Advanced Story Problems

Unit 15: Patterns and Algebra: Patterns and Equality

Unit 16: Geometry: 3-D Shapes

Unit 17: Measurement: Time, Area, and Capacity

Unit 18: Probability and Data Management: Collecting Data and Probability Words

Counting by 5s

☐ Count by 5s. Fill in the blanks.

5,　10,　15,　20,　25,　_____,　35,　40

5,　10,　15,　_____,　25,　30,　35,　40

40,　45,　50,　55,　60,　65,　_____,　75,　80

25, 30, _____

35, 40, _____

75, 80, _____

10, _____, 20

40, _____, 50

70, _____, 80

30, 35, _____

10, 15, _____

65, _____, 75

90, _____, 100

55, _____, 65

30, _____, 40

Counting Groups of 5

How many?

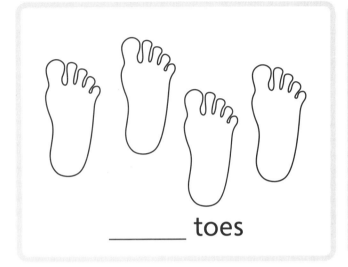

_____ toes

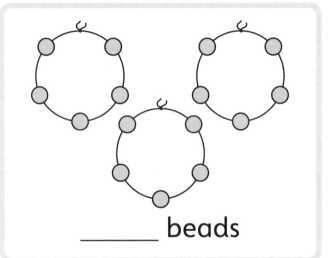

_____ beads

_____ pencils

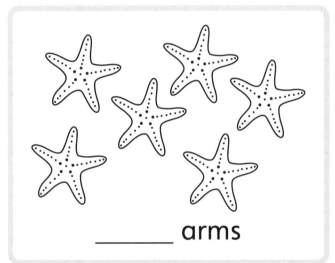

_____ arms

_____ birds

☐ Use groups of 5 to count.

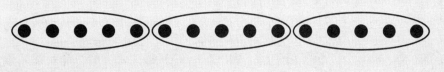

_5, 10, 15_

_____

_____

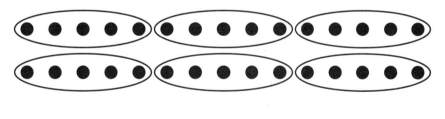

_____

Bonus: Make groups of 5 to count.

_____

Counting by 5s and 1s

⬜ Group by 5s and then by 1s.

_5, 10, 15, 16_

_____

_____

_____

_____

Bonus

_____

☐ Count by 5s and then by Is to see how many.

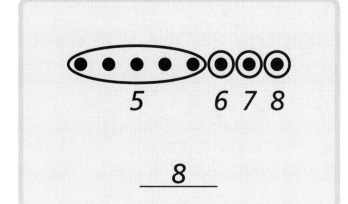

5   6 7 8

_____8_____

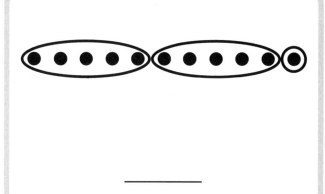

_____

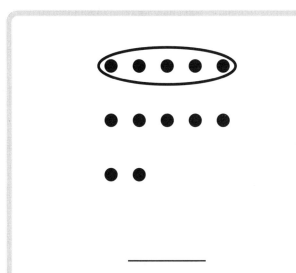

_____

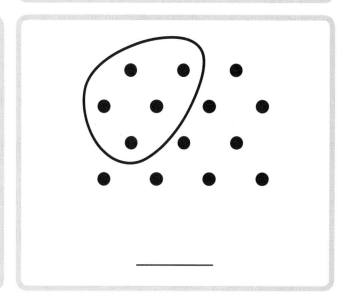

_____

_____

_____

Counting by 2s

☐ Start at 2 and count by 2s.
☐ Colour the numbers that you say.

1	2	3	4	5	6	7	8	9	10
11	12	13	14	15	16	17	18	19	20
21	22	23	24	25	26	27	28	29	30

☐ Count by 2s. Fill in the blanks.

2,   4,   _____,   _____,   10,

12,   14,   16,   _____,   20,

22,   _____,   _____,   28,   30

2,   4,   6,   8,   _____,

12,   _____,   _____,   18,   20,

22,   24,   26,   _____,   _____,

_____,   _____,   36,   _____,   40

Counting by Grouping 2s

How many?

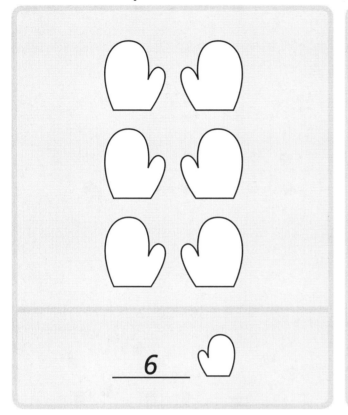

_____6_____

_____

_____

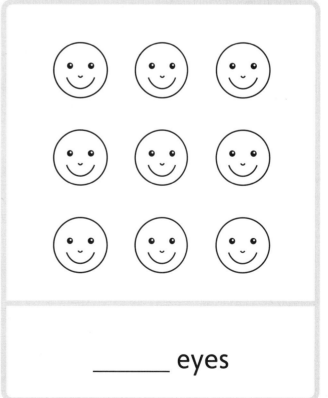

_____ eyes

☐ Count by 2s to see how many dots.

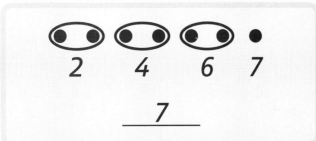

_____

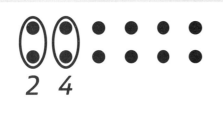

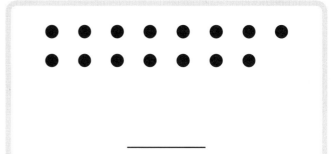

_____

_____

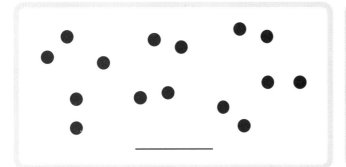

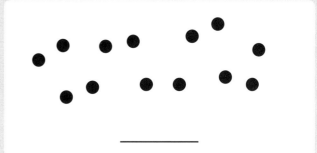

_____

_____

How many letters? Hint: Make groups of 2.

_____

R o s a l i n d

_____

K a p a p a m a h c h a k w e w

_____

Doubles and Skip Counting

☐ Add to double the number.

0 + 0 = _____   1 + 1 = _____   2 + 2 = _____

3 + 3 = _____   4 + 4 = _____   5 + 5 = _____

How did you add? count on / skip count

☐ Draw the same number of dots.
  How many dots are there altogether?

The double of 3 is __6__.

The double of 4 is _____.

The double of 2 is _____.

The double of 5 is _____.

☐ Write the numbers above the number words.
☐ Solve the problem.

3   3
Three bears are brown. Three bears are white.
How many bears altogether? __6__

Jen has four cars. Marko brings four more.
How many cars do they have now? _____

Five children are playing. Five more join them.
Now how many children are playing? _____

Kate sees eight seals and eight birds.
How many animals does she see? _____

Zack is two years old. Don is **double** that.
How old is Don? _____

Grouping in Different Ways

☐ Group by 10s to see how many.

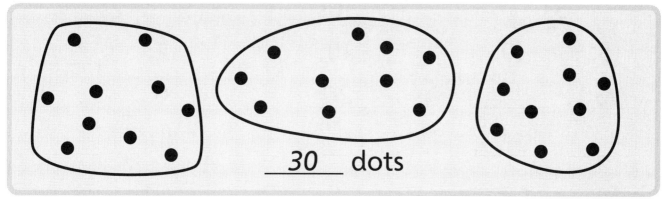

_____30_____ dots

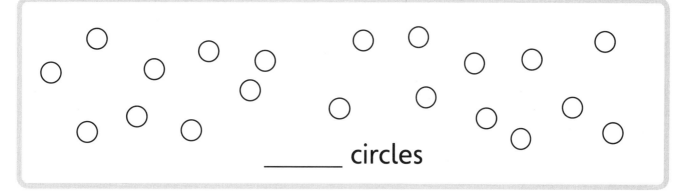

_____ circles

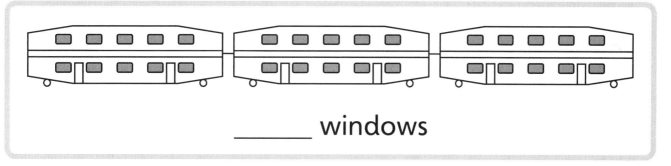

_____ windows

_____ stars

☐ Count by ...

5s	10s	2s
5, 10,	10,	2, _____,
_15_ , _____ ,	_20_ ,	6, _____,
_____ , _30_ ,	_____ ,	10, _____,
_____ , _____ ,	_____	_____ , _____,
_____ , _____		_____ , 20

How many?

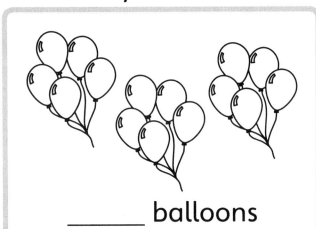

_____ balloons

_____ feet

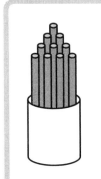 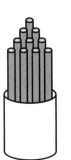 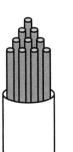 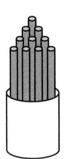 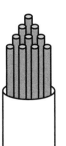 

_____ straws

☐ Count the dots each way. Show the groups.

Count by 2s then Is.

There are _____ dots.

Count by 5s then Is.

There are _____ dots.

Count by 10s then Is.

There are _____ dots.

☐ Did you get the same answer all ways? _____

☐ Circle the faster way to count.

by 2s   by 5s   by 10s

☐ Show 10 in different ways.

10 = __5__ groups of 2 and __0__ more

10 = _____ groups of 3 and _____ more

☐ Now make the groups yourself.

10 = _____ groups of 4 and _____ more

10 = _____ groups of 5 and _____ more

Skip Counting Backwards

☐ Count back by 2s.

1	2	3	4	5	6	7	8	9	10
11	12	13	14	15	16	17	18	19	20

20,   18,   _____,   _____,   _____,   _10_

16,   14,   _____,   _____,   _____,   _____

12,   10,   _____,   _____,   _____,   _____

☐ Count back by 5s.

1	2	3	4	5	6	7	8	9	10
11	12	13	14	15	16	17	18	19	20

20,   _____,   _____,   _____,   _0_

Tens and Ones Blocks

1	2	3	4	5	6	7	8	9	10
11	12	13	14	15	16	17	18	19	20
21	22	23	24	25	26	27	28	29	30

24 is **2** tens blocks and **4** ones blocks.

☐ Fill in the blanks.

1	2	3	4	5	6	7	8	9	10
11	12	13	14	15	16	17	18	19	20
21	22	23	24	25	26	27	28	29	30
31	32	33	34	35	36	37	38	39	40

28 is _____ tens blocks and _____ ones blocks.

35 is _____ tens blocks and _____ ones blocks.

27 is _____ tens blocks and _____ ones blocks.

30 is _____ tens blocks and _____ ones blocks.

23 is _____ tens blocks and _____ ones blocks.

☐ Fill in the chart.
☐ Write the number shown.

tens	ones
3	4

Number ___34___

tens	ones

Number _____

tens	ones

Number _____

tens	ones

Number _____

☐ Show each number using blocks.

| 50 | 43 | 37 | 19 | 32 |

Finding Numbers in a Hundreds Chart

☐ Shade the numbers.

~~1~~ ~~7~~ 8 9 10 11 12 14 15 18 20

21 23 25 28 29 30 31 35 38 40

1	2	3	4	5	6	7	8	9	10
11	12	13	14	15	16	17	18	19	20
21	22	23	24	25	26	27	28	29	30
31	32	33	34	35	36	37	38	39	40

72 73 74 77 79 83

87 88 89 93 97 99

71	72	73	74	75	76	77	78	79	80
81	82	83	84	85	86	87	88	89	90
91	92	93	94	95	96	97	98	99	100

☐ Write the letters you see.

_____ _____ _____ _____

☐ Write the missing numbers.

33	34	35		37
43	44	45	46	47
53	54	55	56	57

11	12	13	14
21	22	23	24
31		33	34

21	22	23
31	32	33
41	42	
51	52	53

64	65	66
	75	76
84	85	86
94	95	

48	49
58	59
	69
78	79

16	17	18	19	20
26	27	28	29	30
36		38	39	40
46	47	48	49	
56	57	58	59	60

Bonus

32		34	35	
42	43	44		46
	53	54	55	56
62	63	64	65	
72	73		75	76

After, Before, and Between

1	2	3	4	5	6	7	8	9	10
11	12	13	14	15	16	17	18	19	20
21	22	23	24	(25)	26	27	28	29	30
31	32	33	34	35	36	37	38	39	40
41	42	43	44	45	46	47	48	49	50

☐ Circle the number on the chart.
☐ Write what comes **after**.
☐ Write what comes **before**.

___24___ , 25, ___26___

_____ , 8, _____

_____ , 37, _____

_____ , 47, _____

_____ , 33, _____

_____ , 19, _____

_____ , 40, _____

_____ , 21, _____

1	2	3	4	5	6	7	8	9	10
11	12	13	14	15	16	17	18	19	20
21	22	23	24	25	26	27	28	29	30
31	32	33	34	35	36	37	38	39	40
41	42	43	44	45	46	47	48	49	50

☐ Place tokens on the two numbers.
☐ Write all the numbers in between.

3, _____, _____, _____, _____, 8

13, _____, _____, _____, _____, 18

43, _____, _____, _____, _____, 48

7, _____, _____, _____, _____, 12

27, _____, _____, _____, _____, 32

Ordering Numbers to 50

How many squares are shaded?

☐ Write the numbers in the blanks.
☐ Circle **more** or **less**.

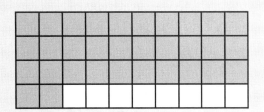 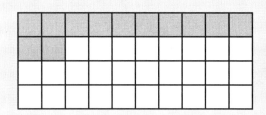

_32_ is (more) / less than _12_ .

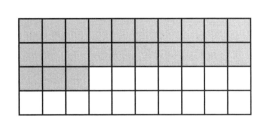 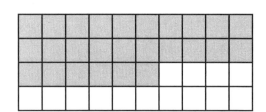

_____ is more / less than _____ .

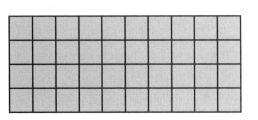 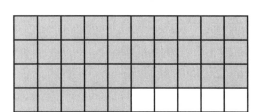

_____ is more / less than _____ .

How many squares are shaded?

☐ Write the numbers in the blanks.
☐ Circle **more** or **less**.

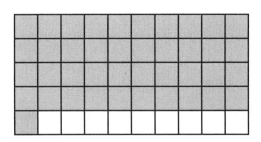 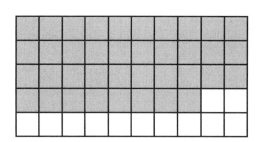

_____ is more / less than _____.

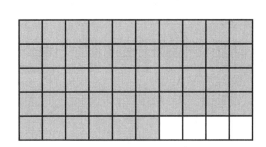 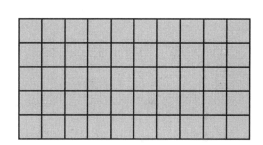

_____ is more / less than _____.

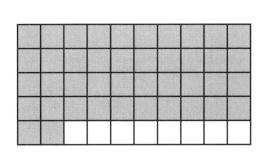 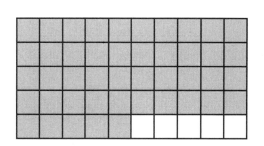

_____ is more / less than _____.

☐ Shade the numbers.
☐ Write them in order.

~~13~~   ~~6~~   11   35   28   40

1	2	3	4	5	6	7	8	9	10
11	12	13	14	15	16	17	18	19	20
21	22	23	24	25	26	27	28	29	30
31	32	33	34	35	36	37	38	39	40

_____, _____, _____, _____, _____, _____

27   10   19   2   28   34   30

1	2	3	4	5	6	7	8	9	10
11	12	13	14	15	16	17	18	19	20
21	22	23	24	25	26	27	28	29	30
31	32	33	34	35	36	37	38	39	40

_____, _____, _____, _____, _____, _____, _____

☐ Place tokens on the chart. Solve the problem.

1	2	3	4	5	6	7	8	9	10
11	12	13	14	15	16	17	18	19	20
21	22	23	24	25	26	27	28	29	30
31	32	33	34	35	36	37	38	39	40

Jay has 35 buttons.

Ben has 21 buttons.

Who has more buttons? _____

Nora picks 26 berries.

Kim picks 34 berries.

Who picks more berries? _____

John has 15 shells, Rob has 36 shells,

and Marko has 28 shells.

Who has the most shells? _____

Identifying Coins

Match each coin with its picture.

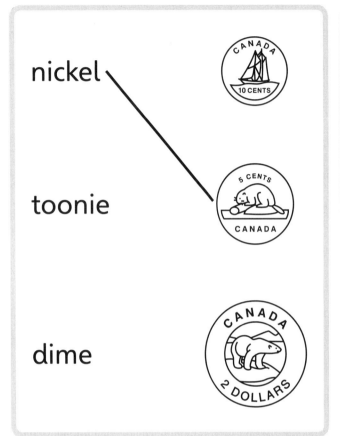

nickel

toonie

dime

loonie

quarter

penny

penny   nickel   dime   quarter   loonie   toonie

Coin Values

Write the value on the coin.

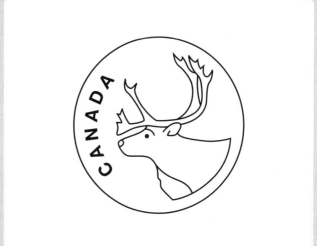

☐ Circle the coin that is worth more.

☐ Circle the coin that is worth the most.

Number Sense 1-62

How Much Money?

☐ Write how much.

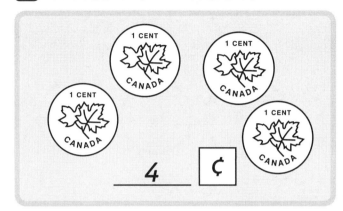

_____4_____ ¢

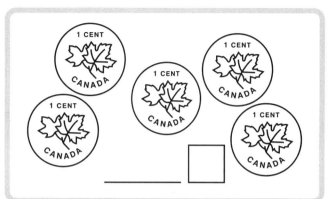

_____ ☐

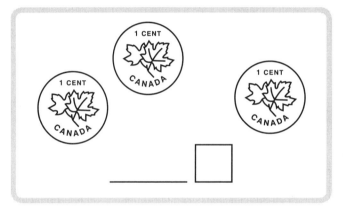

_____ ☐

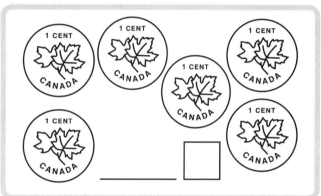

_____ ☐

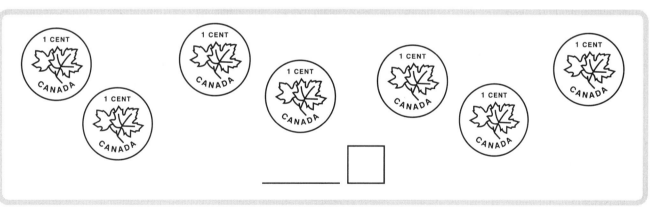

_____ ☐

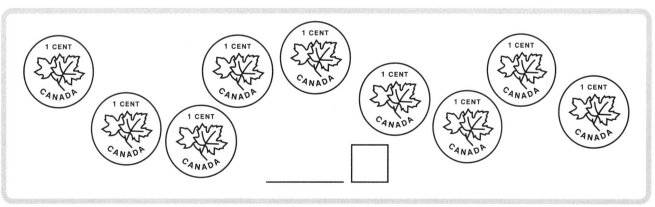

_____ ☐

Emma trades 5 pennies for a nickel.

☐ Draw Emma's money.

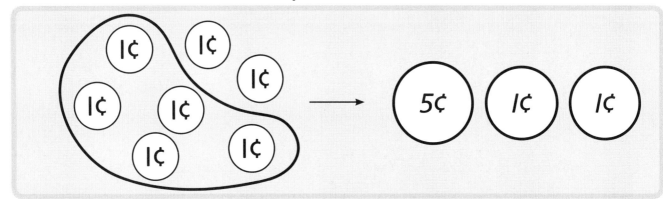

☐ Count by 5s and then by 1s.
  How much money does Emma have?

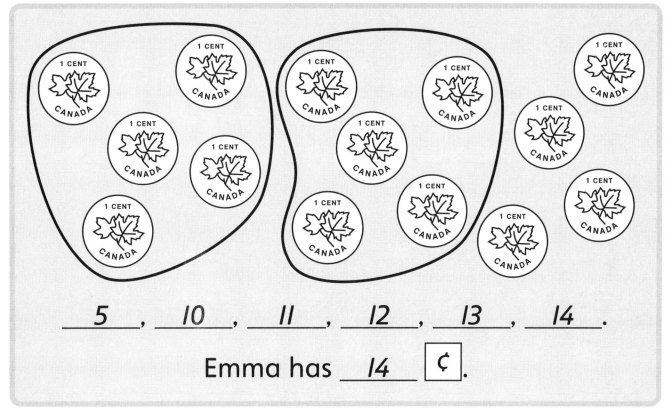

___5___ , ___10___ , ___11___ , ___12___ , ___13___ , ___14___ .

Emma has ___14___ | ¢ | .

_____ , _____ , _____ , _____ , _____ .

Emma has _____ ☐ .

Add the money.

☐ Count by Is.

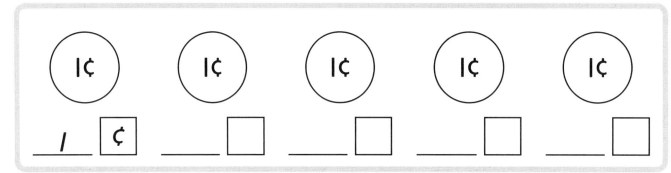

☐ Count by 5s.

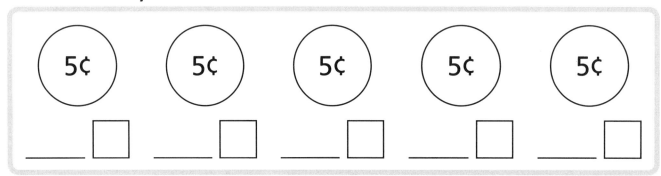

☐ Count by 5s and then by Is.

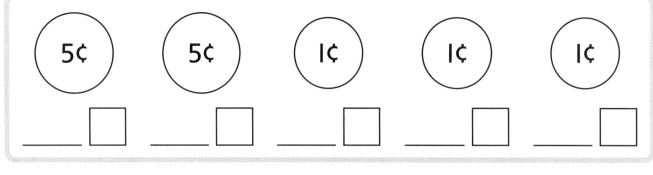

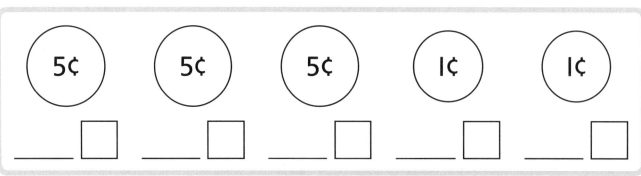

Does Cody have enough money?

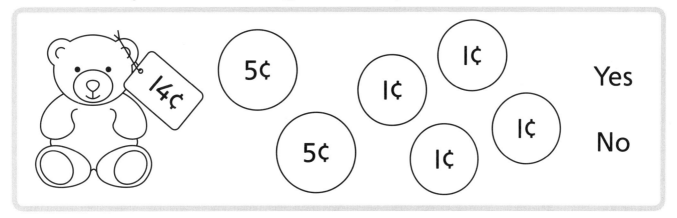

Yes

No

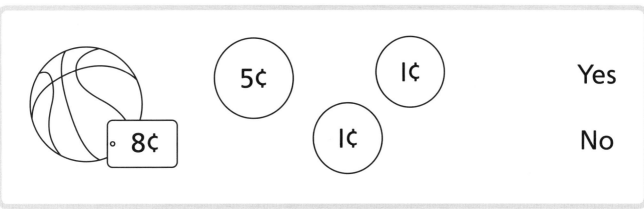

Yes

No

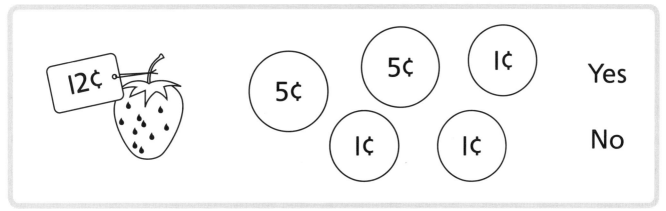

Yes

No

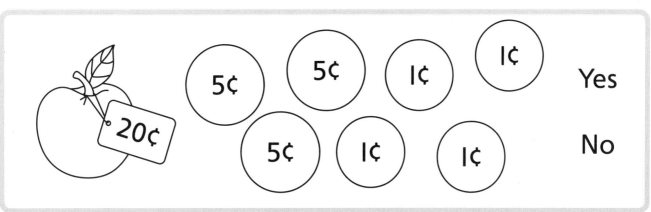

Yes

No

Adding and Subtracting Money

☐ Add the money.

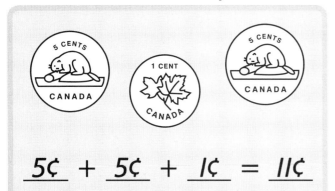

$\underline{5}¢ + \underline{5}¢ + \underline{1}¢ = \underline{11}¢$

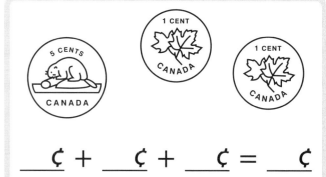

$\underline{}¢ + \underline{}¢ + \underline{}¢ = \underline{}¢$

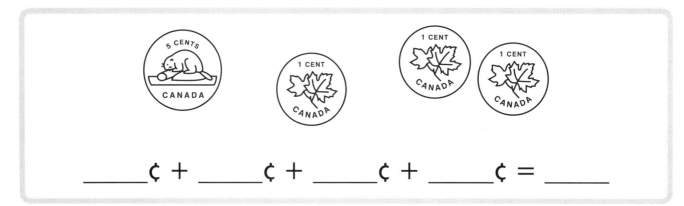

$\underline{}¢ + \underline{}¢ + \underline{}¢ + \underline{}¢ = \underline{}$

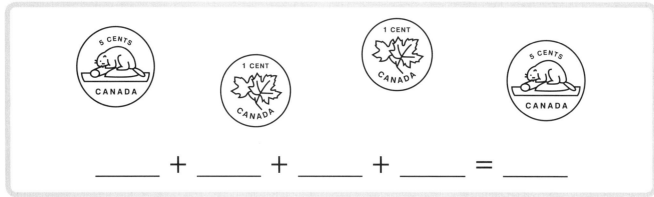

$\underline{} + \underline{} + \underline{} + \underline{} = \underline{}$

$\underline{} + \underline{} + \underline{} + \underline{} + \underline{} + \underline{} = \underline{}$

☐ Solve the problem.

Lily pays 6 cents for a book and 2 cents for a pen. How much money does she spend altogether?

Aki sells an apple for 3 cents and an orange for 1 cent. How much money does she get in total?

Ronin has 5 cents. He buys a sticker for 3 cents. How much money does he have left?

Bonus

A teddy bear costs 8 cents. Jack pays with a dime. How much change does he get?

Number Lines

The frog starts at 0.

☐ Number each jump.
☐ Circle the number the frog stops at.

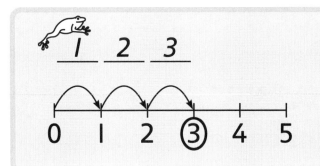

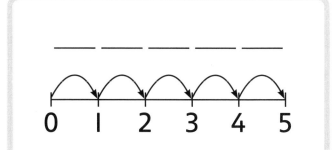

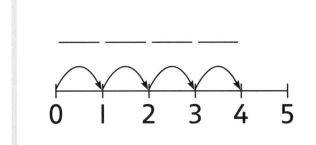

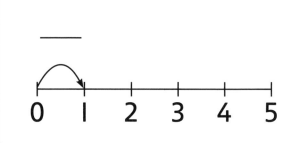

☐ Show the number on the number line.

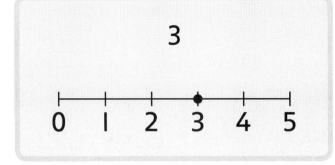

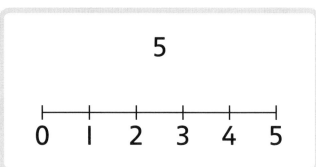

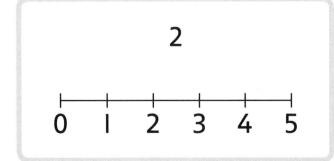

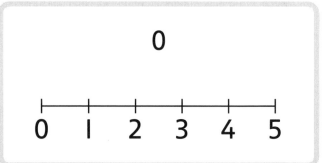

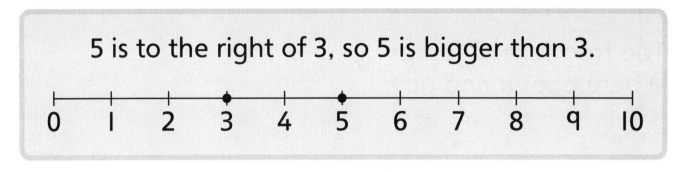

5 is to the right of 3, so 5 is bigger than 3.

☐ Show the numbers on the number line.
☐ Circle the bigger number.

2 and 5

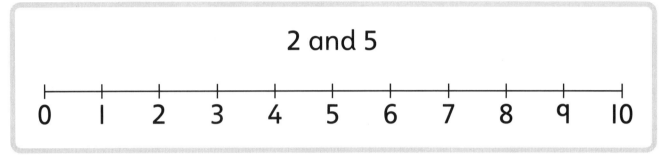

7 and 4

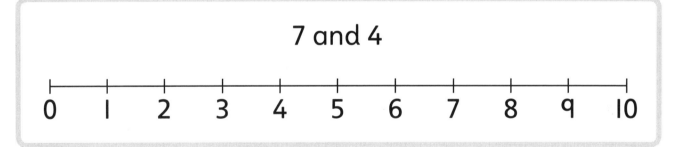

9 and 6

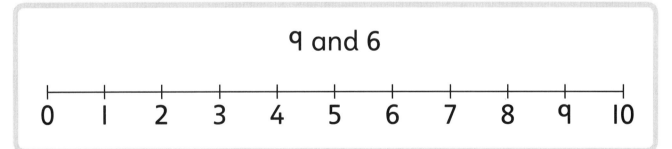

0 and 10

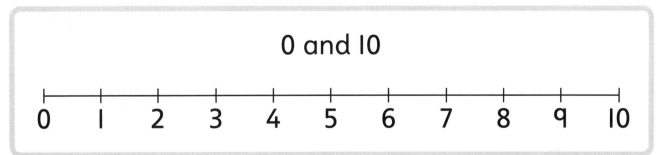

Using Number Lines to Add

The frog takes 2 jumps.
Where does it end up?

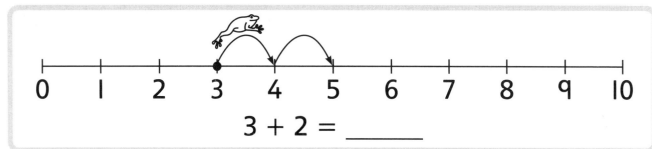

$$3 + 2 = \underline{\hspace{2cm}}$$

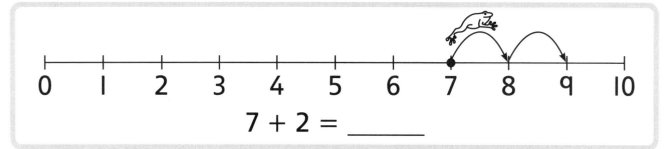

$$7 + 2 = \underline{\hspace{2cm}}$$

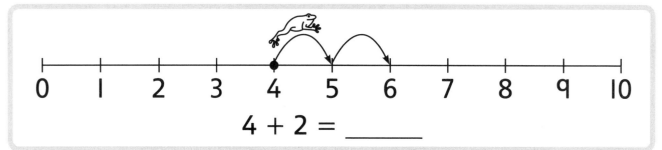

$$4 + 2 = \underline{\hspace{2cm}}$$

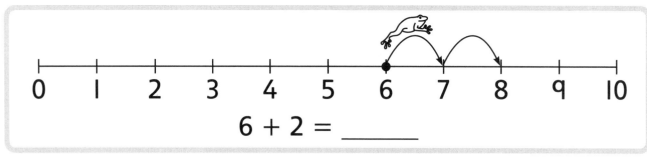

$$6 + 2 = \underline{\hspace{2cm}}$$

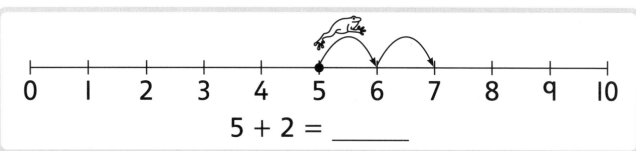

$$5 + 2 = \underline{\hspace{2cm}}$$

☐ Trace the jumps.
☐ Add.

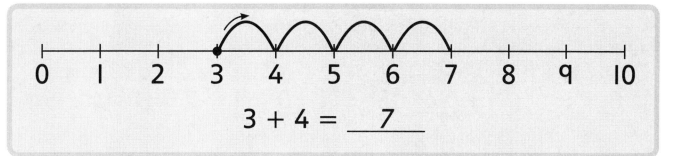

$3 + 4 =$ ____7____

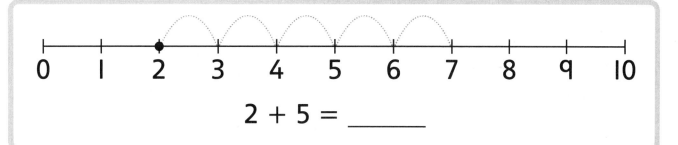

$2 + 5 =$ _____

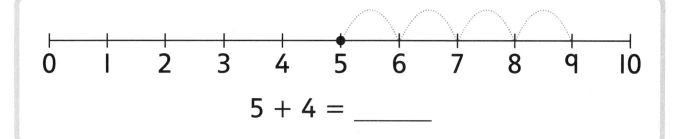

$5 + 4 =$ _____

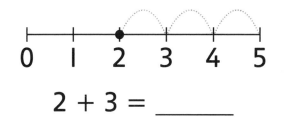

$2 + 3 =$ _____

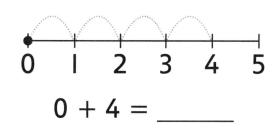

$0 + 4 =$ _____

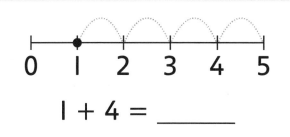

$1 + 4 =$ _____

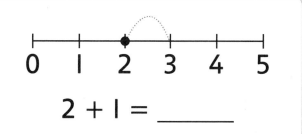

$2 + 1 =$ _____

☐ Count the jumps.
☐ Fill in the blank.

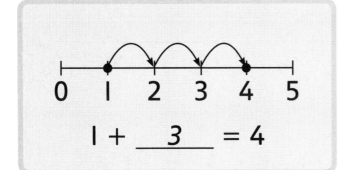

1 + ___3___ = 4

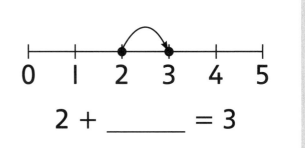

2 + _____ = 3

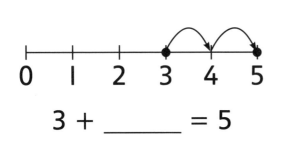

3 + _____ = 5

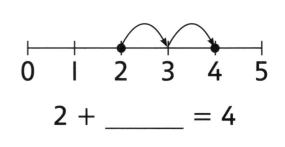

2 + _____ = 4

☐ Trace the correct number of jumps.
☐ Add.

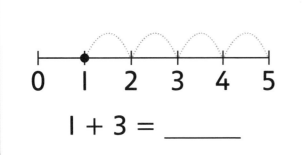

1 + 3 = _____

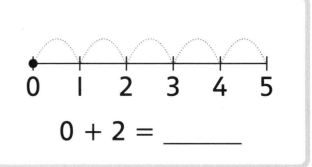

0 + 2 = _____

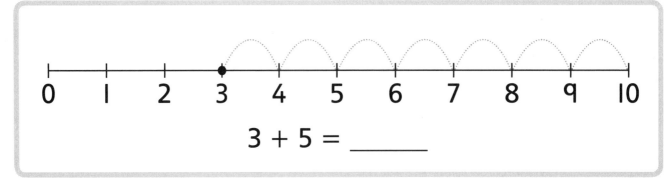

3 + 5 = _____

☐ Match the dots to the addition sentence.

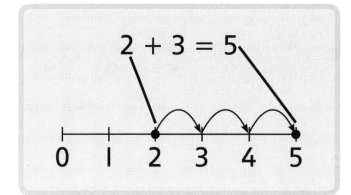

$2 + 3 = 5$

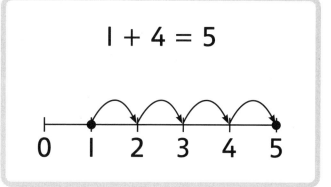

$1 + 4 = 5$

$1 + 2 = 3$

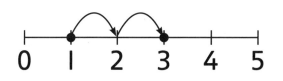

$2 + 1 = 3$

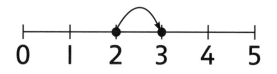

☐ Fill in the blanks.

$\underline{\ \ 1\ \ } + 3 = \underline{\ \ 4\ \ }$

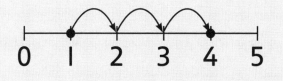

$\underline{\ \ \ \ } + 3 = \underline{\ \ \ \ }$

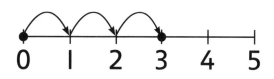

$\underline{\ \ \ \ } + 1 = \underline{\ \ \ \ }$

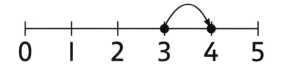

$\underline{\ \ \ \ } + 2 = \underline{\ \ \ \ }$

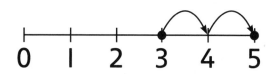

☐ Use the number line to add.

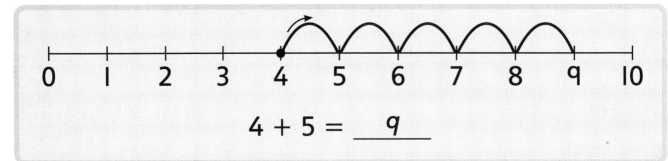

4 + 5 = ___9___

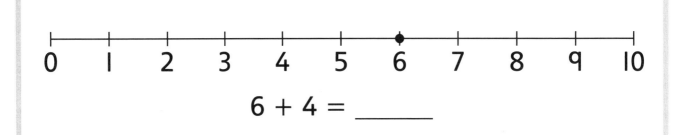

6 + 4 = _____

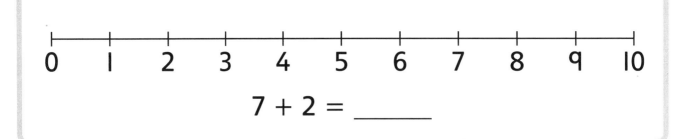

7 + 2 = _____

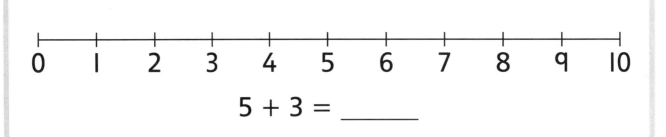

5 + 3 = _____

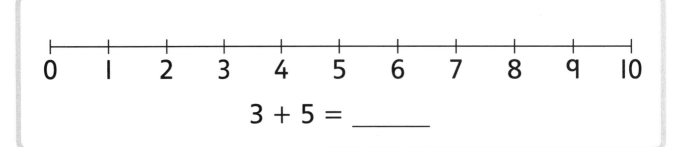

3 + 5 = _____

Subtracting 1 or 2

☐ Take away the last circle.
☐ Subtract 1.

1   2   3   4
○   ○   ○   ⊗

$4 - 1 = \underline{\quad 3 \quad}$

1   2   3   4   5
○   ○   ○   ○   ⊗

$5 - 1 = \underline{\quad\quad}$

1   2   3   4   5   6
○   ○   ○   ○   ○   ○

$6 - 1 = \underline{\quad\quad}$

1   2   3   4   5   6   7
○   ○   ○   ○   ○   ○   ○

$7 - 1 = \underline{\quad\quad}$

1   2   3   4   5   6   7   8   9   10
○   ○   ○   ○   ○   ○   ○   ○   ○   ○

$10 - 1 = \underline{\quad\quad}$

1   2   3   4   5   6   7   8
○   ○   ○   ○   ○   ○   ○   ○

$8 - 1 = \underline{\quad\quad}$

☐ Draw I jump back.
☐ Subtract I.

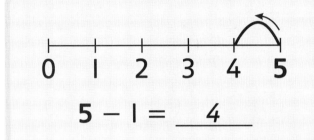

$5 - 1 = \underline{\quad 4 \quad}$

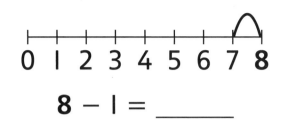

$8 - 1 = \underline{\qquad}$

0   I   2   3   4   5   **6**   7

$6 - 1 = \underline{\qquad}$

0   I   2   3   **4**   5   6   7

$4 - 1 = \underline{\qquad}$

0   I   2   3   4   5   6   7   8   **9**   10   II

$9 - 1 = \underline{\qquad}$

0   I   2   3   4   5   6   7   8   9   **10**   II

$10 - 1 = \underline{\qquad}$

☐ Subtract.

$3 - 1 = \underline{\qquad}$

$7 - 1 = \underline{\qquad}$

Bonus

$14 - 1 = \underline{\qquad}$

☐ Draw 2 jumps back.
☐ Subtract 2.

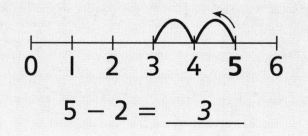

5 − 2 = ___3___

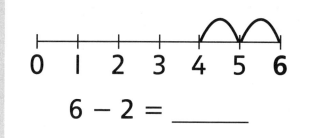

6 − 2 = _____

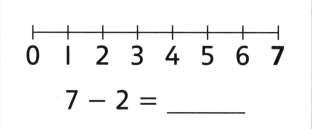

7 − 2 = _____

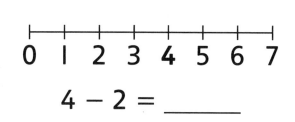

4 − 2 = _____

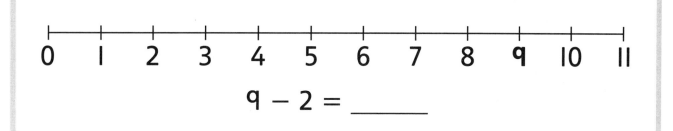

9 − 2 = _____

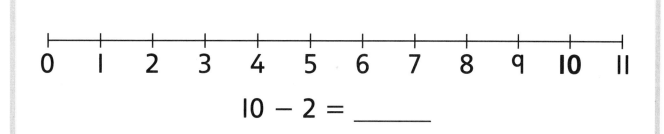

10 − 2 = _____

☐ Subtract.

3 − 2 = ____

8 − 2 = ____

Bonus

15 − 2 = ____

Subtracting on a Number Line (I)

☐ Trace the jumps. Start at the dot.
☐ Count the jumps.

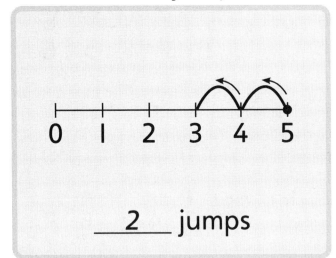

___2___ jumps

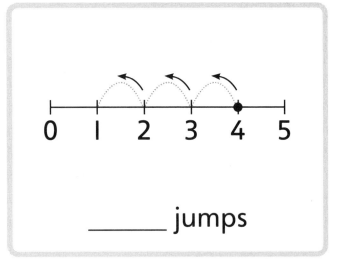

_____ jumps

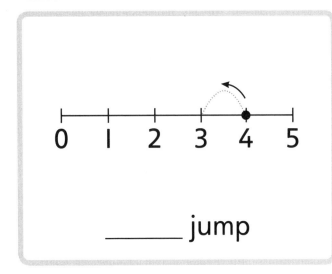

_____ jump

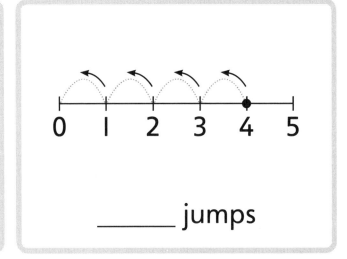

_____ jumps

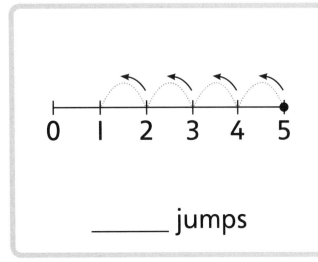

_____ jumps

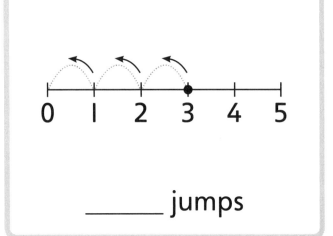

_____ jumps

☐ Fill in the blanks.

The frog took ___3___ jumps.

It stopped at ___1___.

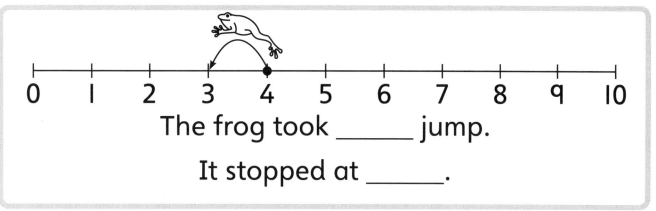

The frog took _____ jump.

It stopped at _____.

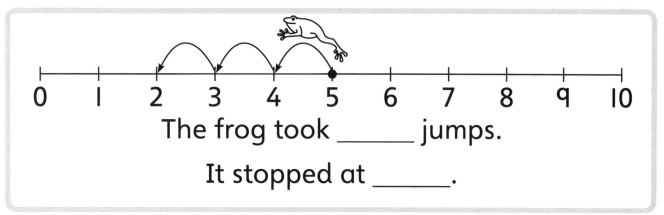

The frog took _____ jumps.

It stopped at _____.

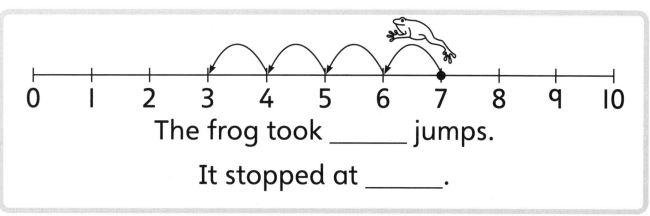

The frog took _____ jumps.

It stopped at _____.

The frog took 2 jumps backwards.

☐ Trace the 2 jumps.
What number did the frog stop at?

The frog stopped
at ___/___ .

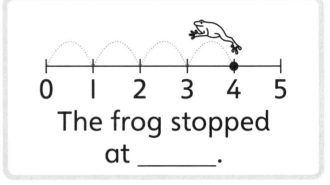

The frog stopped
at _____ .

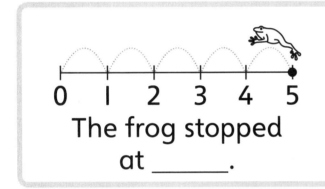

The frog stopped
at _____ .

The frog stopped
at _____ .

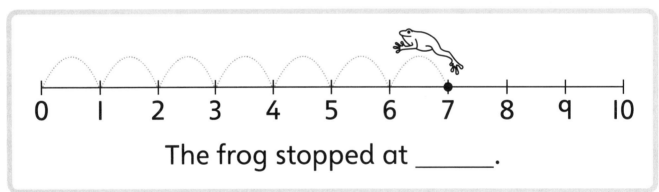

The frog stopped at _____ .

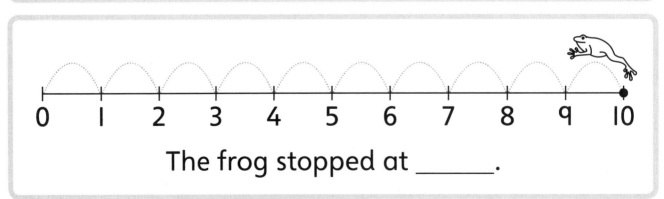

The frog stopped at _____ .

☐ Trace 4 jumps back. Start at the dot.
☐ Subtract 4.

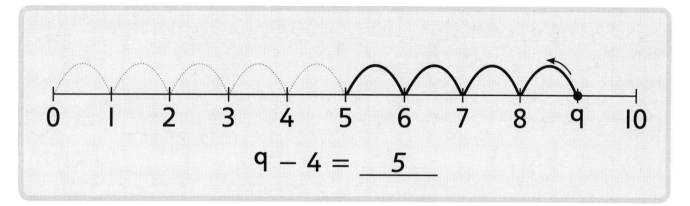

$$9 - 4 = \underline{\quad 5 \quad}$$

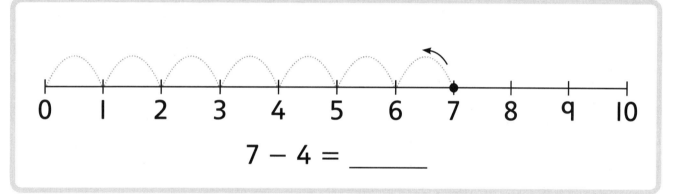

$$7 - 4 = \underline{\qquad}$$

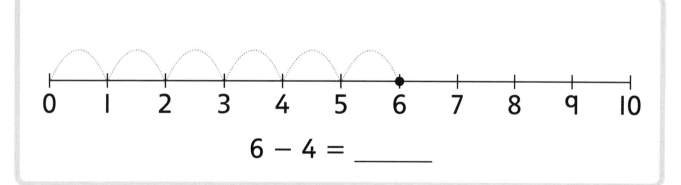

$$6 - 4 = \underline{\qquad}$$

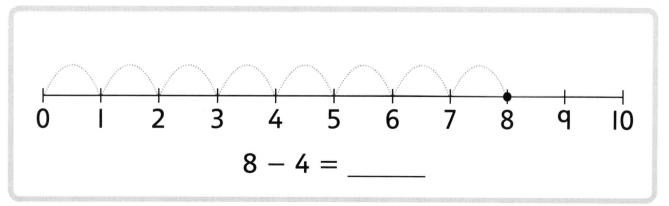

$$8 - 4 = \underline{\qquad}$$

The frog starts at 9.
How many jumps should the frog take?

9 – 4	9 – 3	9 – 6
__4__ jumps	_____ jumps	_____ jumps

☐ How many jumps should the frog take?
Trace the correct number of jumps.

5 – 2

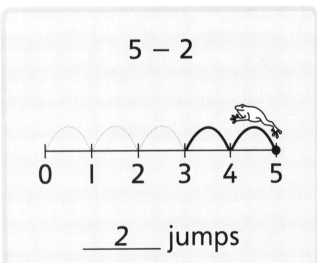

__2__ jumps

4 – 3

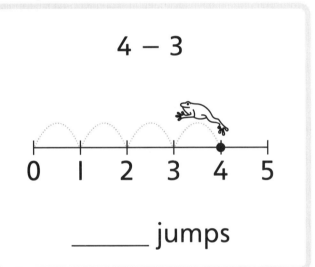

_____ jumps

3 – 1

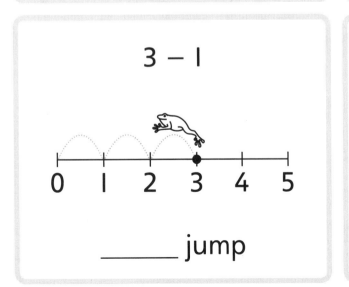

_____ jump

5 – 4

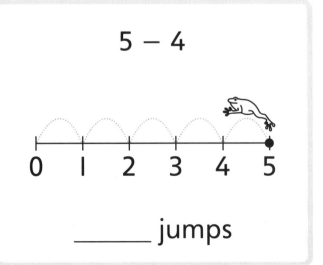

_____ jumps

Subtracting on a Number Line (2)

☐ Trace the correct number of jumps. Start at the dot.
☐ Fill in the blanks.

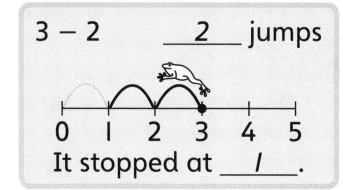

3 − 2 ___2___ jumps

It stopped at ___1___.

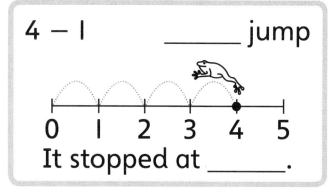

4 − 1 _____ jump

It stopped at _____.

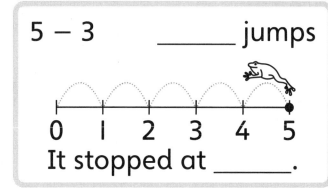

5 − 3 _____ jumps

It stopped at _____.

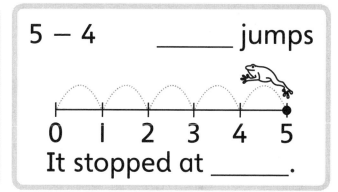

5 − 4 _____ jumps

It stopped at _____.

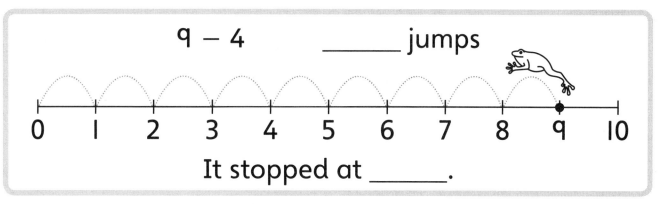

9 − 4 _____ jumps

It stopped at _____.

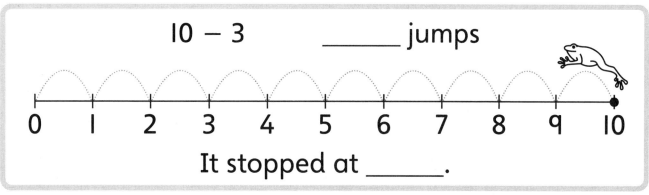

10 − 3 _____ jumps

It stopped at _____.

☐ Trace the correct number of jumps back.
   Start at the dot.
☐ Subtract.

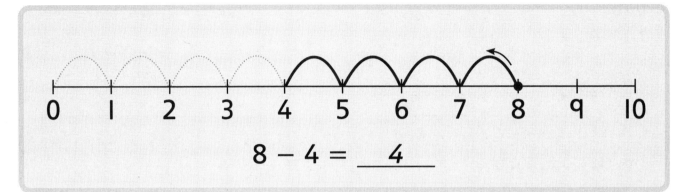

$$8 - 4 = \underline{\quad 4 \quad}$$

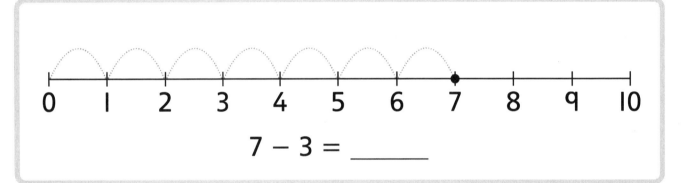

$$7 - 3 = \underline{\qquad}$$

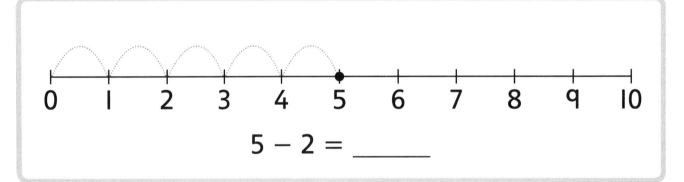

$$5 - 2 = \underline{\qquad}$$

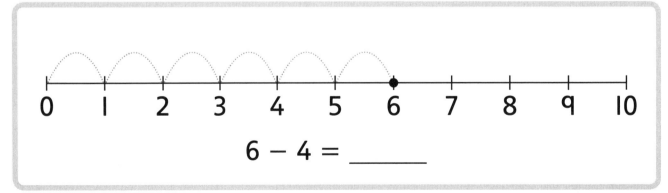

$$6 - 4 = \underline{\qquad}$$

☐ Show where to start tracing.
☐ Trace 5 jumps back.
☐ Subtract.

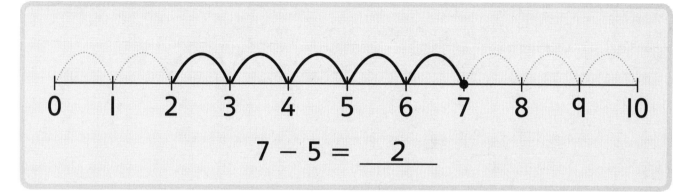

$$7 - 5 = \underline{\ \ 2\ \ }$$

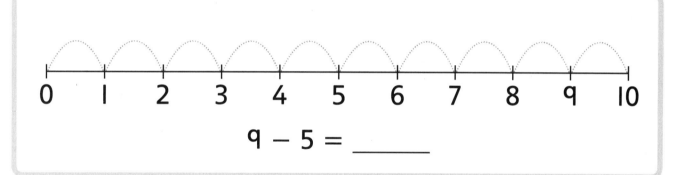

$$9 - 5 = \underline{\hspace{2cm}}$$

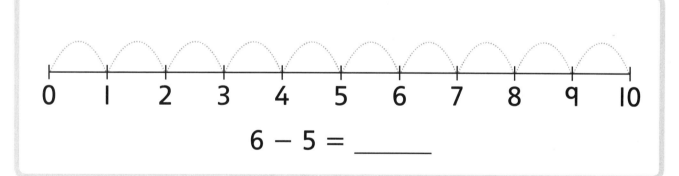

$$6 - 5 = \underline{\hspace{2cm}}$$

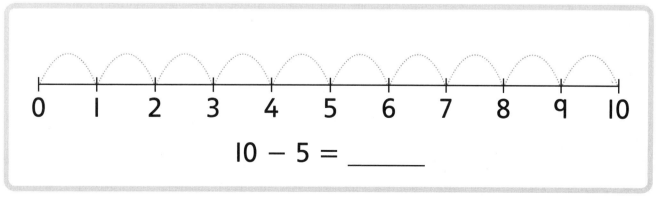

$$10 - 5 = \underline{\hspace{2cm}}$$

☐ Show where to start tracing.
☐ Trace the correct number of jumps back.
☐ Subtract.

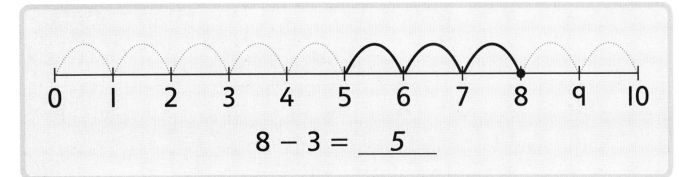

$$8 - 3 = \underline{\quad 5 \quad}$$

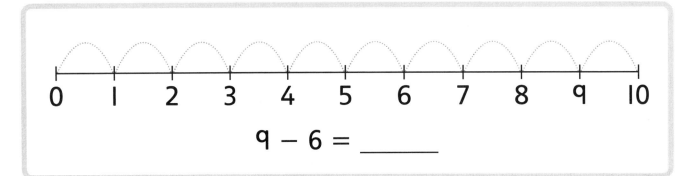

$$9 - 6 = \underline{\qquad}$$

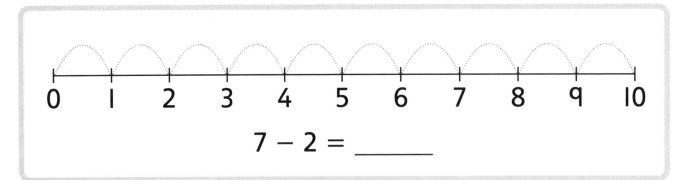

$$7 - 2 = \underline{\qquad}$$

☐ Now write the answer on the left.

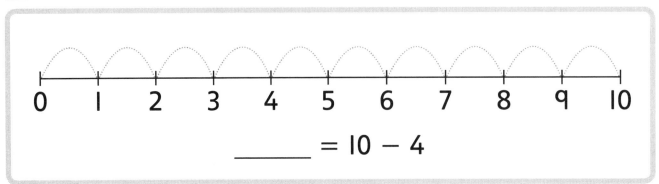

$$\underline{\qquad} = 10 - 4$$

☐ Add or subtract using the number line.

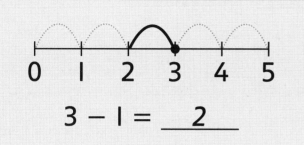

3 − 1 = ___2___

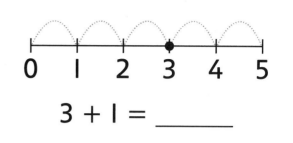

3 + 1 = _____

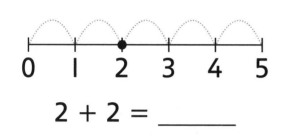

2 + 2 = _____

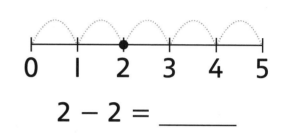

2 − 2 = _____

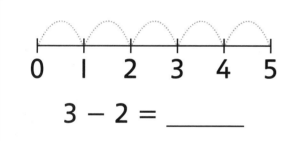

3 − 2 = _____

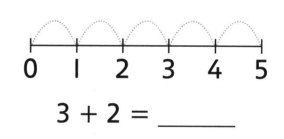

3 + 2 = _____

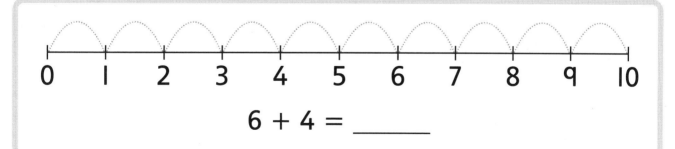

6 + 4 = _____

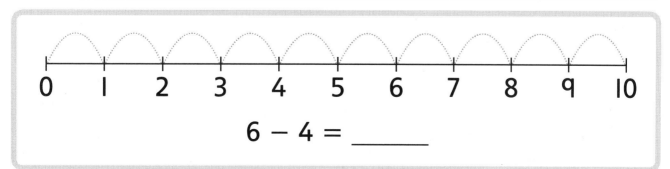

6 − 4 = _____

Counting Back

☐ Write the number that comes **after**.

13 _14_	14 ___	19 ___	18 ___	12 ___
11 ___	10 ___	17 ___	15 ___	16 ___

☐ Write the number that comes **before**.

_12_ 13 14 15 16	___ 14 15 16 17	___ 16 17 18 19
___ 12 13	___ 16 17	___ 13 14	___ 15 16

☐ Write the number that comes **after**.
☐ Write the number that comes **before**.

_17_ 18 _19_	__ 17 __	__ 15 __	__ 13 __
__ 14 __	__ 19 __	__ 12 __	__ 16 __

☐ Write the number that comes before.

__7__ 8 9	_____ 4 5	_____ 2 3
_____ 18 19	_____ 14 15	_____ 12 13
_____ 6 7	_____ 17 18	_____ 3 4
_____ 16 17	_____ 11 12	_____ 19 20
_____ 13 14	_____ 5 6	_____ 1 2
_____ 10 11	_____ 15 16	_____ 9 10

Counting Back to Subtract

5   _4_   _3_ $5 - 2 = \underline{\quad 3 \quad}$

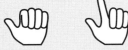

4   _____ _____ _____ $4 - 3 = \underline{\qquad}$

6   _____ _____ _____ $6 - 4 = \underline{\qquad}$

7   _____ _____ _____ $7 - 3 = \underline{\qquad}$

8   _____ _____ $8 - 2 = \underline{\qquad}$

$5 - 3 = \underline{\qquad}$ $6 - 3 = \underline{\qquad}$ $7 - 4 = \underline{\qquad}$

Closer to 0, 10, or 20?

☐ Is it closer to 0 or 10? Write **0** or **10**.

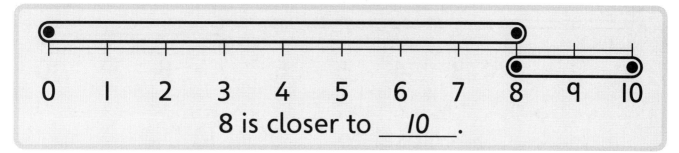

8 is closer to ___10___ .

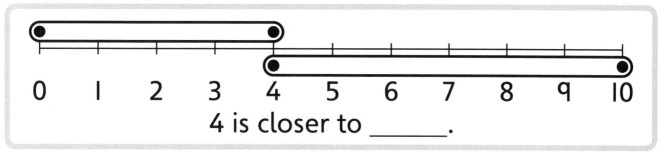

4 is closer to _____ .

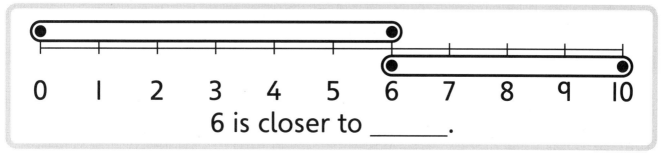

6 is closer to _____ .

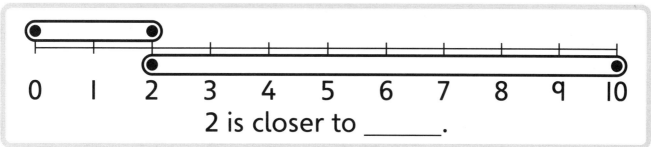

2 is closer to _____ .

☐ **Bonus:** Show that 5 is **equally** close to 0 and 10.

◻ Circle 0, 10, or 20.

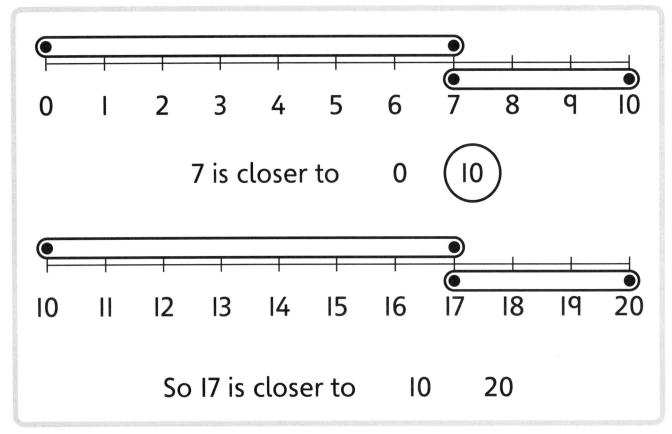

7 is closer to   0   (10)

So 17 is closer to   10   20

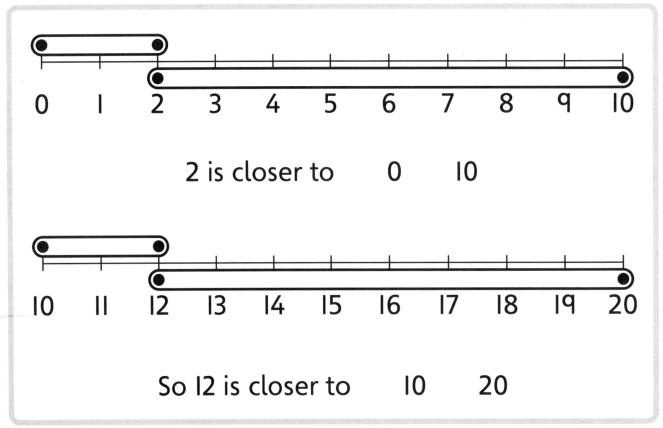

2 is closer to   0   10

So 12 is closer to   10   20

Closer to 0, 5, or 10?

☐ Is it closer to 0 or 5? Write **0** or **5**.

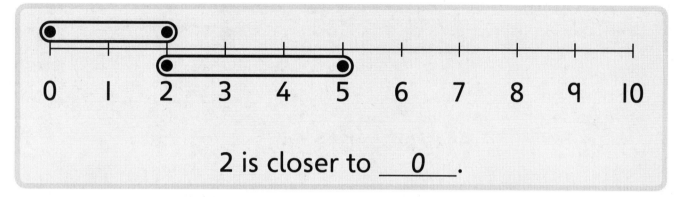

2 is closer to ___0___.

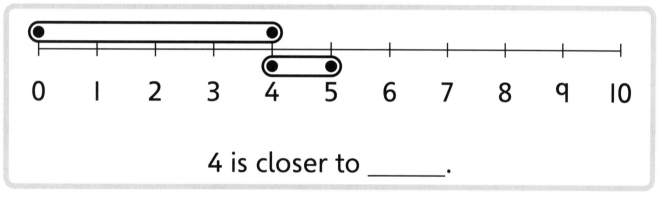

4 is closer to _____.

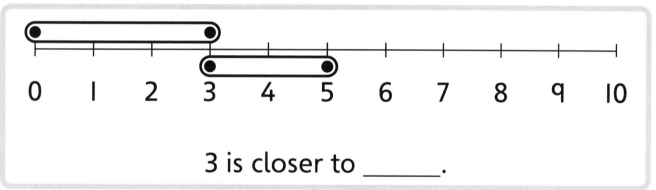

3 is closer to _____.

☐ Now draw the dots yourself.

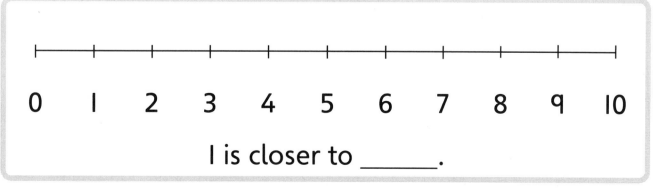

1 is closer to _____.

☐ Is it closer to 5 or 10? Write **5** or **10**.

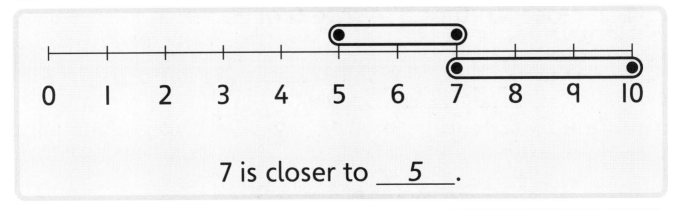

7 is closer to __5__.

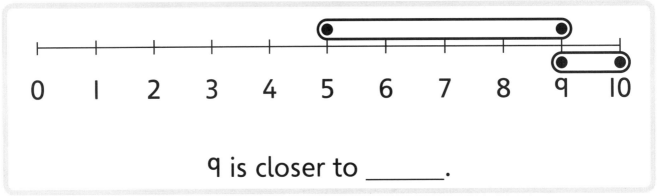

9 is closer to _____.

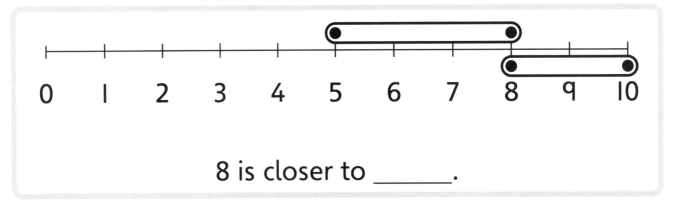

8 is closer to _____.

☐ Now draw the dots yourself.

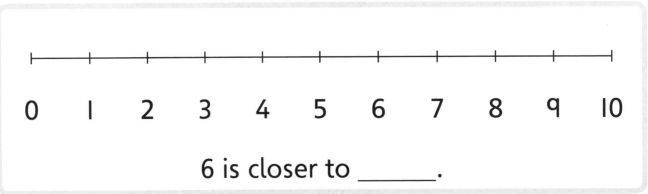

6 is closer to _____.

Estimating How Many

Is it closer to 0, 5, or 10? Guess, then check.

Guess	Count to check
closer to __10__ stars	___9___ stars closer to __10__
closer to _____ stars	_____ stars closer to _____
closer to _____ stars	_____ star closer to _____
closer to _____ stars	_____ stars closer to _____

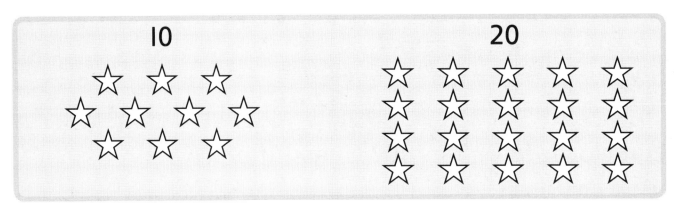

10   **20**

Closer to 10 or 20? Write **10** or **20**.

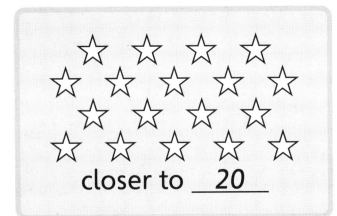

closer to __20__

closer to _____

closer to _____

closer to _____

closer to _____

Pairs Adding to 5

☐ Write the missing numbers.

 $\boxed{3}$ + $\boxed{2}$ = 5

fingers up   fingers down   altogether

 $\boxed{}$ + $\boxed{}$ = 5

fingers up   finger down   altogether

 $\boxed{}$ + $\boxed{}$ = 5

finger up   fingers down   altogether

 $\boxed{}$ + $\boxed{}$ = 5

fingers up   fingers down   altogether

3 + 2 = 5

fingers up   fingers not up   altogether

☐ Hold up the correct number of fingers.
How many are not up?

$1 + \boxed{} = 5$

$4 + \boxed{} = 5$

$\begin{array}{r} 2 \\ + \boxed{} \\ \hline 5 \end{array}$

$\begin{array}{r} \boxed{} \\ + \quad 1 \\ \hline 5 \end{array}$

$\begin{array}{r} \boxed{} \\ + \quad 3 \\ \hline 5 \end{array}$

$\begin{array}{r} 5 \\ + \boxed{} \\ \hline 5 \end{array}$

$5 - 1 = \boxed{}$

$5 - 2 = \boxed{}$

$\boxed{} = 5 - 3$

$5 - 5 = \boxed{}$

Addition Facts

☐ Add by remembering.

2 + 3 = _____

1 + 2 = _____

4 + 1 = _____

2 + 1 = _____

1 + 1 = _____

3 + 2 = _____

3 + 3 = _____

1 + 4 = _____

1 + 3 = _____

3 + 1 = _____

2 + 2 = _____

4 + 4 = _____

5 + 5 = _____

Bonus

2 + 1 + 2 = _____

Subtraction Facts

☐ Subtract by remembering.

3 − 2 = _____

2 − 1 = _____

4 − 1 = _____

4 − 2 = _____

5 − 2 = _____

5 − 1 = _____

5 − 4 = _____

4 − 3 = _____

5 − 3 = _____

3 − 1 = _____

2 − 2 = _____

6 − 3 = _____

8 − 4 = _____

10 − 5 = _____

Using 5 to Add

☐ Circle the two numbers that make 5.

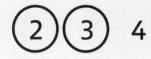 ②③ 4	1 3 4	1 2 3
1 2 4	4 1 3	3 4 2

☐ Circle the two numbers that make 5.
☐ Write the number that is left over.

②+③+ 4 = 5 + $\boxed{4}$

4 + 1 + 3 = 5 + $\boxed{}$

3 + 1 + 4 = 5 + $\boxed{}$

0 + 3 + 5 = 5 + $\boxed{}$

4 + 3 + 2 = 5 + $\boxed{}$

☐ Circle the two numbers that make 5.
☐ Use 5 to add.

$4 + 1 + 3$

$= 5 + \boxed{3}$

$= \boxed{8}$

$2 + 3 + 4$

$= 5 + \boxed{}$

$= \boxed{}$

$3 + 1 + 4$

$= 5 + \boxed{}$

$= \boxed{}$

$3 + 4 + 2$

$= 5 + \boxed{}$

$= \boxed{}$

$2 + 4 + 3$

$= 5 + \boxed{}$

$= \boxed{}$

$3 + 1 + 2$

$= 5 + \boxed{}$

$= \boxed{}$

$1 + 2 + 3$

$= 5 + \boxed{}$

$= \boxed{}$

$2 + 1 + 4$

$= 5 + \boxed{}$

$= \boxed{}$

$4 + 3 + 1$

$= 5 + \boxed{}$

$= \boxed{}$

$4 + 3 + 2 = \boxed{}$

$4 + 2 + 1 = \boxed{}$

$3 + 2 + 1 = \boxed{}$

$3 + 4 + 1 = \boxed{}$

Pairs Adding to 10

How many are unshaded? How many are shaded?

◯ Fill in the addition sentence.

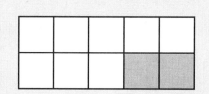

___8___ + ___2___ = 10

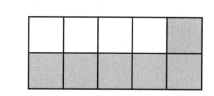

_____ + _____ = 10

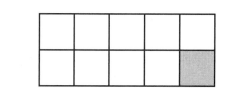

_____ + _____ = 10

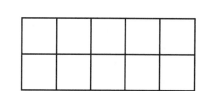

_____ + _____ = 10

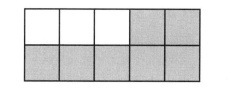

_____ + _____ = 10

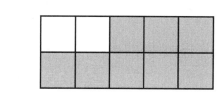

_____ + _____ = 10

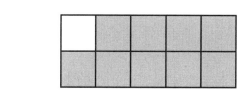

_____ + _____ = 10

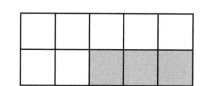

_____ + _____ = 10

  7 + 3 = 10

up   not up   altogether

☐ Hold up the correct number of fingers.
How many are not up?

$4 + \boxed{} = 10$

$5 + \boxed{} = 10$

$$\begin{array}{r} 8 \\ + \boxed{} \\ \hline 10 \end{array}$$

$$\begin{array}{r} 3 \\ + \boxed{} \\ \hline 10 \end{array}$$

$$\begin{array}{r} \boxed{} \\ + \quad 9 \\ \hline 10 \end{array}$$

$$\begin{array}{r} 10 \\ + \boxed{} \\ \hline 10 \end{array}$$

$10 - 3 = \boxed{}$

$10 - 2 = \boxed{}$

$\boxed{} = 10 - 4$

$10 - 5 = \boxed{}$

Using 10 to Add

☐ Circle the two numbers that make 10.

④ 5 ⑥	3 7 9	1 8 9
4 5 5	2 3 8	3 6 4

☐ Circle the two numbers that make 10.
☐ Write the number that is left over.

⑧ + ② + 5 = 10 + ⟦ 5 ⟧

4 + 6 + 3 = 10 + ☐

2 + 9 + 1 = 10 + ☐

6 + 7 + 4 = 10 + ☐

4 + 3 + 7 = 10 + ☐

☐ Circle the two numbers that make 10.
☐ Use 10 to add.

(8) + 3 + (2)
= 10 + [3]
= [13]

2 + 7 + 3
= 10 + ☐
= ☐

1 + 8 + 9
= 10 + ☐
= ☐

3 + 7 + 4
= 10 + ☐
= ☐

4 + 5 + 6
= 10 + ☐
= ☐

5 + 5 + 6
= 10 + ☐
= ☐

9 + 2 + 1
= 10 + ☐
= ☐

3 + 2 + 8
= 10 + ☐
= ☐

4 + 5 + 5
= 10 + ☐
= ☐

8 + 4 + 2
= 10 + ☐
= ☐

7 + 3 + 9
= 10 + ☐
= ☐

6 + 4 + 8
= 10 + ☐
= ☐

Making 10 to Add

☐ Use the group of 10 to help you add.

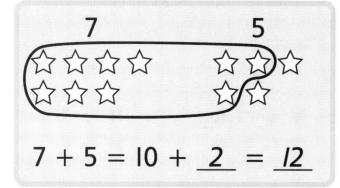

7   5

$7 + 5 = 10 + \underline{\ 2\ } = \underline{\ 12\ }$

8   6

$8 + 6 = 10 + \underline{\ \ \ } = \underline{\ \ \ }$

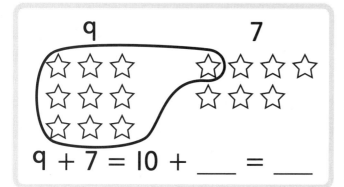

9   7

$9 + 7 = 10 + \underline{\ \ \ } = \underline{\ \ \ }$

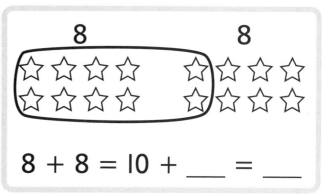

8   8

$8 + 8 = 10 + \underline{\ \ \ } = \underline{\ \ \ }$

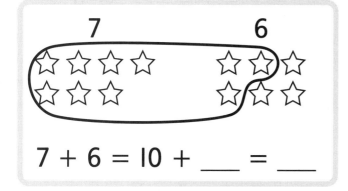

7   6

$7 + 6 = 10 + \underline{\ \ \ } = \underline{\ \ \ }$

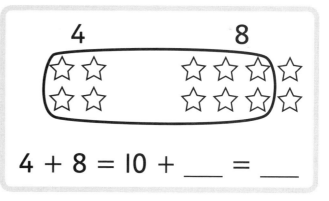

4   8

$4 + 8 = 10 + \underline{\ \ \ } = \underline{\ \ \ }$

Yu groups 10 in two ways. Are the answers the same?

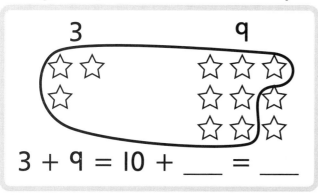

3   9

$3 + 9 = 10 + \underline{\ \ \ } = \underline{\ \ \ }$

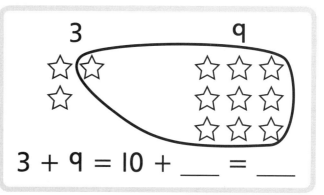

3   9

$3 + 9 = 10 + \underline{\ \ \ } = \underline{\ \ \ }$

☐ Circle a group of 10.
☐ Use 10 to add.

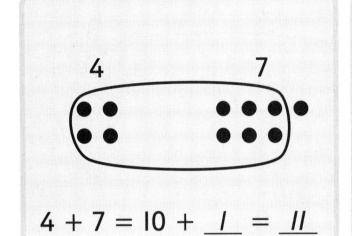

4   7

$4 + 7 = 10 + \underline{\;I\;} = \underline{\;II\;}$

8   6

$8 + 6 = 10 + \underline{\;\;\;} = \underline{\;\;\;}$

9   4

$9 + 4 = 10 + \underline{\;\;\;} = \underline{\;\;\;}$

9   2

$9 + 2 = 10 + \underline{\;\;\;} = \underline{\;\;\;}$

7   7

$7 + 7 = 10 + \underline{\;\;\;} = \underline{\;\;\;}$

Draw the dots.
6   9

$6 + 9 = 10 + \underline{\;\;\;} = \underline{\;\;\;}$

Patterns in Adding

☐ Colour the correct number of hearts.
☐ Finish the addition sentence.

$0 + \boxed{4} = 4$ ♡ ♡ ♡ ♡

coloured   not coloured

$1 + \boxed{} = 4$ ♥ ♡ ♡ ♡

coloured   not coloured

$2 + \boxed{} = 4$ ♡ ♡ ♡ ♡

coloured   not coloured

$3 + \boxed{} = 4$ ♡ ♡ ♡ ♡

coloured   not coloured

$4 + \boxed{} = 4$ ♡ ♡ ♡ ♡

coloured   not coloured

As the number of ♥ goes up by 1,

the number of ♡ goes _____.

COPYRIGHT © 2017 JUMP MATH: NOT TO BE COPIED

☐ Complete the addition sentence.

| | 0 | + | 5 | = | 5 |

| | 1 | + | ☐ | = | ☐ |

| | ☐ | + | ☐ | = | ☐ |

| | ☐ | + | ☐ | = | ☐ |

| | ☐ | + | ☐ | = | ☐ |

| | ☐ | + | ☐ | = | ☐ |

Which number is the same every time? _____

As the 1st number goes up by 1,

the 2nd number _____.

One More, One Less

$3 + 2 = 5$

so $4 + 2 = \underline{6}$

○○○ ○○
●○○○ ○○

$7 + 3 = 10$

so $8 + 3 = \underline{}$

○○○○○○○ ○○○
●○○○○○○ ○○○

$8 + 2 = 10$

so $9 + 2 = \underline{}$

○○○○○○○ ○○
●○○○○○○○ ○○

$6 + 4 = 10$

so $6 + 5 = \underline{}$

○○○○○○ ○○○○
○○○○○○ ●○○○○

$4 + 1 = 5$

so $4 + 2 = \underline{}$

$6 + 4 = 10$

so $7 + 4 = \underline{}$

$5 + 6 = \underline{}$

$3 + 3 = \underline{}$

$7 + 3 = 10$

so $7 + 2 = \underline{\quad 9 \quad}$

$\bigcirc\bigcirc\bigcirc\bigcirc\bigcirc\bigcirc\bigcirc \quad \bigcirc\bigcirc\bigcirc$

$\bigcirc\bigcirc\bigcirc\bigcirc\bigcirc\bigcirc\bigcirc \quad \otimes\bigcirc\bigcirc$

$3 + 2 = 5$

so $3 + 1 = \underline{\qquad}$

$\bigcirc\bigcirc\bigcirc \quad \bigcirc\bigcirc$

$\bigcirc\bigcirc\bigcirc \quad \otimes\bigcirc$

$6 + 4 = 10$

so $5 + 4 = \underline{\qquad}$

$\bigcirc\bigcirc\bigcirc\bigcirc\bigcirc\bigcirc \quad \bigcirc\bigcirc\bigcirc\bigcirc$

$\bigcirc\bigcirc\bigcirc\bigcirc\bigcirc\otimes \quad \bigcirc\bigcirc\bigcirc\bigcirc$

$4 + 1 = 5$

so $4 + 0 = \underline{\qquad}$

$\bigcirc\bigcirc\bigcirc\bigcirc \quad \bigcirc$

$\bigcirc\bigcirc\bigcirc\bigcirc \quad \otimes$

$5 + 5 = 10$

so $4 + 5 = \underline{\qquad}$

$2 + 3 = 5$

so $2 + 2 = \underline{\qquad}$

$4 + 1 = 5$

so $3 + 1 = \underline{\qquad}$

$5 + 5 = 10$

so $5 + 4 = \underline{\qquad}$

6 + 4 = 10

so 6 + 3 = _____   ○○○○○○ ○○○○

○○○○○○ ○○○⊗

6 + 4 = 10

so 5 + 4 = _____   ○○○○○○ ○○○○

○○○○○⊗ ○○○○

7 + 3 = 10

so 7 + 4 = _____   ○○○○○○○ ○○○

○○○○○○○ ●○○○

7 + 3 = 10

so 7 + 2 = _____

7 + 3 = 10

so 6 + 3 = _____

5 + 5 = 10

so 5 + 6 = _____

5 + 5 = 10

so 4 + 5 = _____

8 + 3 = _____

2 + 9 = _____

Pairs Adding to 20

☐ Complete the addition sentences.

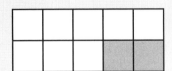

8 + __2__ = 10   so   8 + __12__ = 20

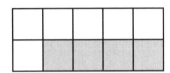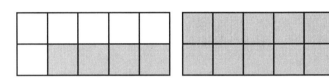

6 + _____ = 10   so   6 + _____ = 20

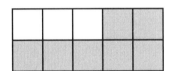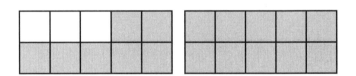

3 + _____ = 10   so   3 + _____ = 20

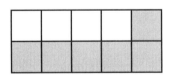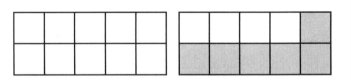

4 + _____ = 10   so   14 + _____ = 20

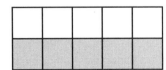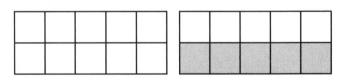

5 + _____ = 10   so   15 + _____ = 20

☐ Complete the addition sentences.

$7 + \underline{\quad 3 \quad} = 10$

so $7 + \underline{\quad 13 \quad} = 20$

$9 + \underline{\quad 1 \quad} = 10$

so $19 + \underline{\quad 1 \quad} = 20$

$5 + \underline{\qquad} = 10$

so $5 + \underline{\qquad} = 20$

$2 + \underline{\qquad} = 10$

so $12 + \underline{\qquad} = 20$

$4 + \underline{\qquad} = 10$

so $14 + \underline{\qquad} = 20$

$6 + \underline{\qquad} = 10$

so $6 + \underline{\qquad} = 20$

$6 + \underline{\qquad} = 10$

so $16 + \underline{\qquad} = 20$

$3 + \underline{\qquad} = 10$

so $13 + \underline{\qquad} = 20$

☐ Complete the addition sentence.

$9 + \underline{\quad 11 \quad} = 20$

$8 + \underline{\qquad} = 20$

$5 + \underline{\qquad} = 20$

$1 + \underline{\qquad} = 20$

Doubles within 20

8 is 5 + 3

so the double of 8

is 10 + __6__ = __16__

● ● ● ● ●   ○ ○ ○
● ● ● ● ●   ○ ○ ○
● ● ● ● ●   ○ ○ ○

6 is 5 + 1

so the double of 6

is 10 + ____ = ____

● ● ● ● ●   ○
● ● ● ● ●   ○
● ● ● ● ●   ○

7 is 5 + 2

so the double of 7

is 10 + ____ = ____

● ● ● ● ●   ○ ○
● ● ● ● ●   ○ ○
● ● ● ● ●   ○ ○

10 is 5 + 5

so the double of 10

is 10 + ____ = ____

● ● ● ● ● ○ ○ ○ ○ ○
● ● ● ● ● ○ ○ ○ ○ ○
● ● ● ● ● ○ ○ ○ ○ ○

9 is 5 + 4

so the double of 9

is 10 + ____ = ____

● ● ● ● ●   ○ ○ ○ ○
● ● ● ● ●   ○ ○ ○ ○
● ● ● ● ●   ○ ○ ○ ○

☐ Move up a row to fill in the blank.

1	2	3	4	5
6	7	8	9	10

$10 = 5 + \underline{\hspace{1.5cm}}$

$7 = 5 + \underline{\hspace{1.5cm}}$

$9 = 5 + \underline{\hspace{1.5cm}}$

$6 = 5 + \underline{\hspace{1.5cm}}$

☐ Double the number using 5 and 10.

$9 = 5 + \underline{\ \ 4\ \ }$

so the double of 9

is $10 + \underline{\ \ 8\ \ } = \underline{\ \ 18\ \ }$

$7 = 5 + \underline{\hspace{1.5cm}}$

so the double of 7

is $10 + \underline{\hspace{1.5cm}} = \underline{\hspace{1.5cm}}$

$6 = 5 + \underline{\hspace{1.5cm}}$

so the double of 6

is $10 + \underline{\hspace{1.5cm}} = \underline{\hspace{1.5cm}}$

$8 = 5 + \underline{\hspace{1.5cm}}$

so the double of 8

is $10 + \underline{\hspace{1.5cm}} = \underline{\hspace{1.5cm}}$

$10 = 5 + \underline{\hspace{1.5cm}}$

so the double of 10

is $10 + \underline{\hspace{1.5cm}} = \underline{\hspace{1.5cm}}$

$11 = 5 + \underline{\hspace{1.5cm}}$

so the double of 11

is $10 + \underline{\hspace{1.5cm}} = \underline{\hspace{1.5cm}}$

Using Doubles to Add

☐ Double and then add 1.

$$4 + 4 + 1 = \boxed{} \qquad \begin{array}{r} 4 \\ + 5 \\ \hline \end{array}$$

$$3 + 3 + 1 = \boxed{} \qquad \begin{array}{r} 3 \\ + 4 \\ \hline \end{array}$$

$$7 + 7 + 1 = \boxed{} \qquad \begin{array}{r} 8 \\ + 7 \\ \hline \end{array}$$

$$8 + 8 + 1 = \boxed{} \qquad \begin{array}{r} 9 \\ + 8 \\ \hline \end{array}$$

$6 + 6 = $ _____

so $6 + 7 = $ _____

$5 + 5 = $ _____

so $6 + 5 = $ _____

$7 + 7 = $ _____

so $7 + 8 = $ _____

$4 + 4 = $ _____

so $5 + 4 = $ _____

$7 + 6 = $ _____

$8 + 9 = $ _____

$5 + 6 = $ _____

$10 + 9 = $ _____

☐ Solve the problem.

Rani has 8 stickers. Matt has double that number. How many stickers does Matt have?

Amir is 6 years old. Nina is double Amir's age. How old is Nina?

Kim is 5 years old. Glen is double as old as Kim. Sindi is one year younger than Glen. How old is Sindi?

Alex picks 9 strawberries. Jin picks double that. Sally picks one more than Jin. How many does Sally pick?

Halves and Quarters

a **whole** pizza	a pizza cut in **half**
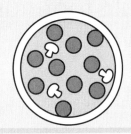	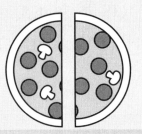

more than half ⟶ ← **less** than half

☐ Write ☺ if the pizza part is **more** than half.
☐ Write ☹ if the pizza part is **less** than half.

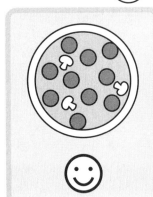	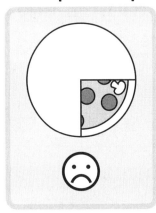	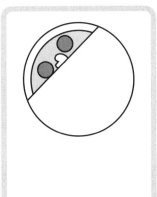	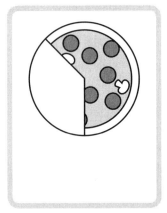
☺	☹		

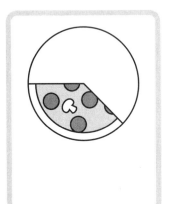	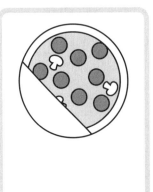	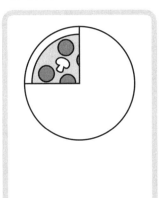	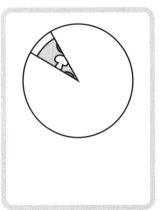

Number Sense 1-87

☐ Circle the pictures that show a half.

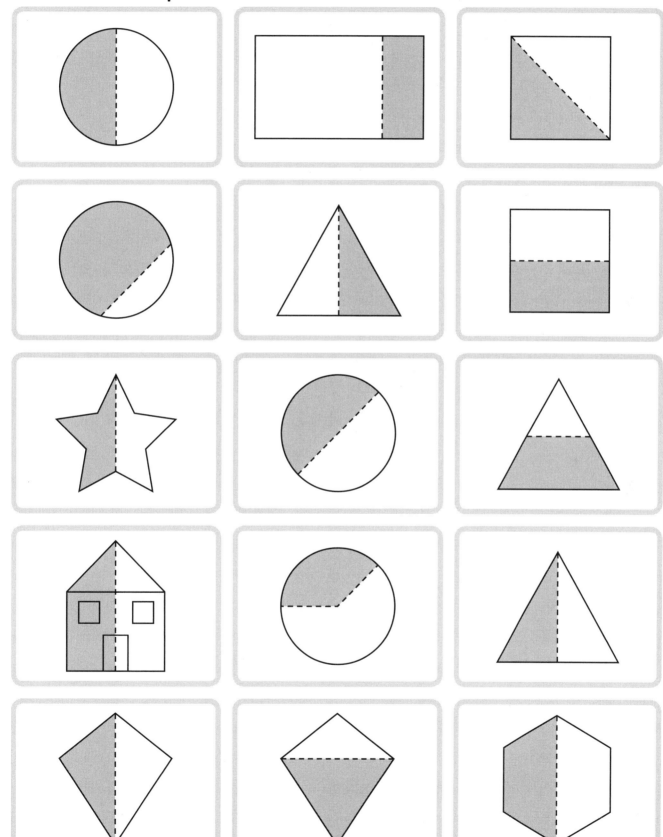

Here are 4 ways to fold a square into **quarters**.

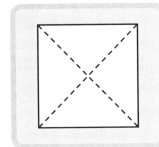 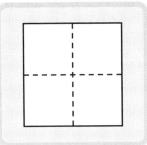 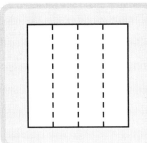 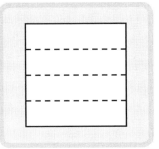

These are **not** quarters.

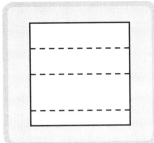 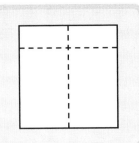 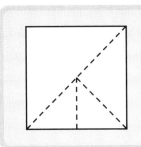 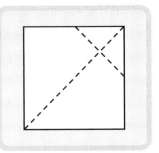

☐ Circle the pictures that show a quarter.

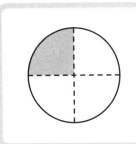 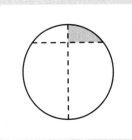 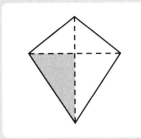 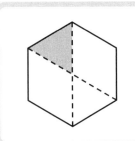

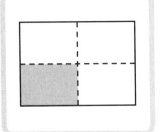 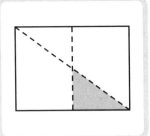 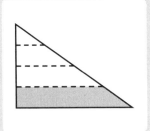 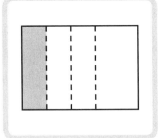

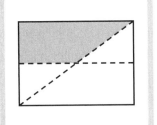 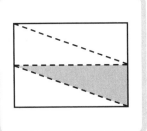 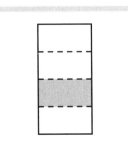 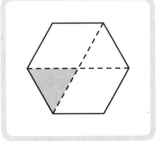

More Than and Fewer Than

☐ Draw circles to show how many.
☐ Fill in the blank.

Matt has 4 stickers.

Sharon has 2 more stickers than Matt.

Matt	◯	◯	◯	◯		
Sharon	◯	◯	◯	◯	◯	◯

Sharon has ___6___ stickers.

Ray has 3 toy boats.

Bella has 4 more toy boats than Ray.

Ray							
Bella							

Bella has _____ toy boats.

Tess eats 2 strawberries.

Kyle eats 4 more strawberries than Tess.

Tess							
Kyle							

Kyle eats _____ strawberries.

☐ Draw ◯ to show how many.
☐ Draw ✗ to show how many fewer.
☐ Fill in the blank.

Jax has **6** stickers.

Emma has **2** fewer stickers than Jax.

| Jax | ◯ | ◯ | ◯ | ◯ | ◯ | ◯ |
| Emma | ◯ | ◯ | ◯ | ◯ | ✗ | ✗ |

Emma has ___4___ stickers.

Karen paints **7** pictures.

Fred paints **3** fewer pictures than Karen.

| Karen | | | | | | | |
| Fred | | | | | | | |

Fred paints _____ pictures.

Sara has **7** books.

John has **3** fewer books than Sara.

| Sara | | | | | | | |
| John | | | | | | | |

John has _____ books.

Ava						
Glen						

☐ Use red cubes for ✕ and blue cubes for ◯.
☐ Fill in the blank.

Ava sees 2 monkeys.

Glen sees 3 more monkeys than Ava.

How many monkeys does Glen see? _____

Ava has 5 shirts.

Glen has 2 fewer shirts than Ava.

How many shirts does Glen have? _____

Ava sees 6 birds.

Glen sees I fewer bird than Ava.

How many birds does Glen see? _____

Ava has **four** pens.

Glen has **two** more pens than Ava.

How many pens does Glen have? _____

How Many More and Adding

☐ Draw more circles.
☐ Write the addition.

2 more than 3

___3___ + ___2___

2 more than 6

___6___ + _____

2 more than 5

_____ + _____

2 more than 7

_____ + _____

5 more than 4

_____ + _____

3 more than 8

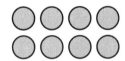

_____ + _____

3 more than 6

_____ + _____

4 more than 3

_____ + _____

☐ Draw more circles.
☐ Write the **addition sentence**.

5 more than 2 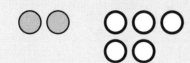 <u> 2 </u> + <u> 5 </u> = <u> 7 </u>	**2 more than 6** ____ + ____ = ____
4 more than 5  ____ + ____ = ____	**6 more than 2** ____ + ____ = ____
2 more than 3 ____ + ____ = ____	**I more than 4** ____ + ____ = ____
three more than **four** ____ + ____ = ____	**four** more than **two** ____ + ____ = ____

☐ Write an addition sentence to find the answer.

3 more than 5

__5__ + __3__ = __8__

3 more than 5 is __8__.

4 more than 6

____ + ____ = ____

4 more than 6 is ____.

6 more than 2

____ + ____ = ____

6 more than 2 is ____.

3 more than 4

____ + ____ = ____

3 more than 4 is ____.

I more than 8

____ + ____ = ____

I more than 8 is ____.

2 more than 10

____ + ____ = ____

2 more than 10 is ____.

7 more than 10

____ + ____ = ____

7 more than 10 is ____.

2 more than 16

____ + ____ = ____

2 more than 16 is ____.

Counting On to Find How Many More

☐ Circle the matching numbers.
☐ Trace the extra numbers.
☐ Fill in the blanks.

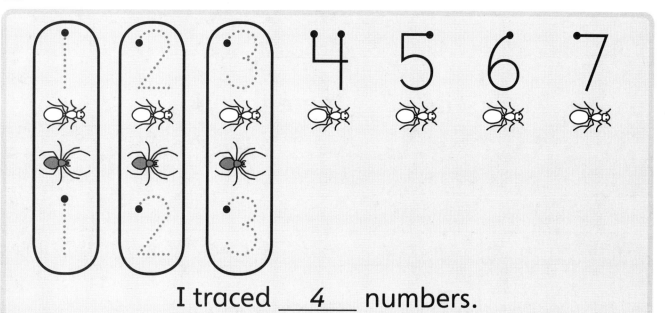

I traced ___4___ numbers.

There are ___4___ more  than .

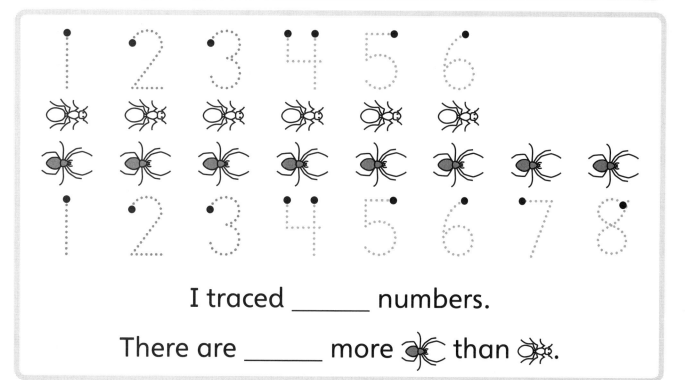

I traced _____ numbers.

There are _____ more  than .

☐ Draw jumps to find how many more.
How many jumps did you draw?

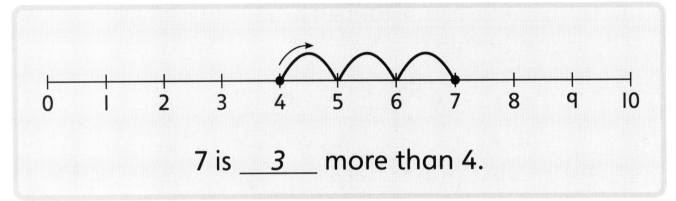

7 is ___3___ more than 4.

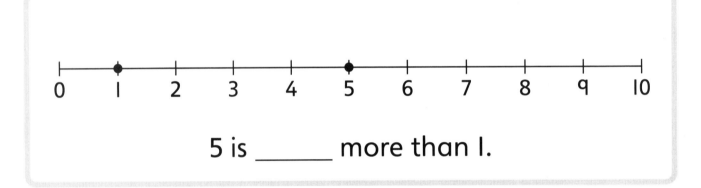

5 is _____ more than I.

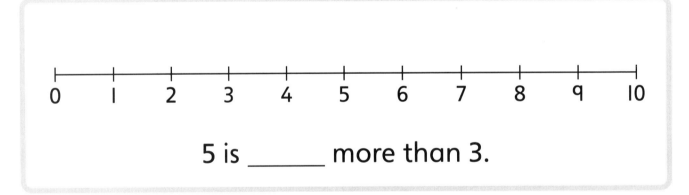

5 is _____ more than 3.

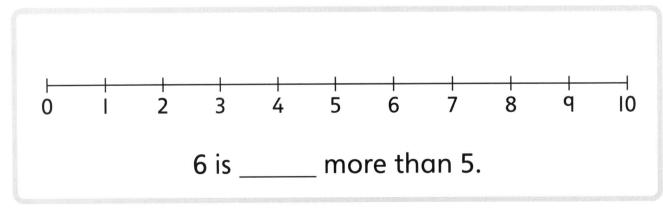

6 is _____ more than 5.

6 is _____ more than 4.

You can count on to find the missing number.

4	5	6
4 is **0** more than 4.	5 is **1** more than 4.	6 is **2** more than 4.

2 fingers are up, so 6 is __2__ more than 4.

9 is _____ more than 6.

8 is _____ more than 3.

9 is _____ more than 7.

6 is _____ more than 3.

7 is _____ more than 5.

3 is _____ more than 1.

5 is _____ more than 0.

4 is _____ more than 1.

Finding a Missing Addend

☐ Draw circles to find the missing number.

$3 + \boxed{2} = 5$

●●● ○○

$2 + \boxed{} = 6$

●●

$1 + \boxed{} = 5$

●

$3 + \boxed{} = 6$

●●●

$4 + \boxed{} = 7$

●●
●●

$5 + \boxed{} = 6$

●●●
●●

$2 + \boxed{} = 5$

●●

$3 + \boxed{} = 7$

●●●

$2 + \boxed{} = 4$

●●

$1 + \boxed{} = 3$

●

Number Sense 1-91

$$4 + \underline{\hspace{2cm}} = 6$$

You can count on to find the missing number.

4	5	6

$$4 + \mathbf{0} = 4 \qquad 4 + \mathbf{1} = 5 \qquad 4 + \mathbf{2} = 6$$

2 fingers are up, so $4 + \underline{\ 2\ } = 6$.

☐ Find the missing number by counting on.

$$4 + \underline{\hspace{2cm}} = 7 \qquad\qquad 5 + \underline{\hspace{2cm}} = 6$$

$$8 + \underline{\hspace{2cm}} = 10 \qquad\qquad 7 + \underline{\hspace{2cm}} = 12$$

$$5 + \underline{\hspace{2cm}} = 10 \qquad\qquad 14 + \underline{\hspace{2cm}} = 16$$

$$11 + \underline{\hspace{2cm}} = 12 \qquad\qquad 17 + \underline{\hspace{2cm}} = 20$$

Bonus

$$35 + \underline{\hspace{2cm}} = 38$$

Bonus

$$98 + \underline{\hspace{2cm}} = 100$$

Addition Problems with an Unknown Change

☐ Solve the first 3 problems.
☐ Use your answers to solve the last problem.

7 children are biking.

1 more joins.

Now how many children are biking? _____

7 children are biking.

2 more join.

Now how many children are biking? _____

7 children are biking.

3 more join.

Now how many children are biking? _____

7 children are biking.

Some more join.

Now 10 children are biking.

How many children joined? _____

☐ Write the addition sentence with a box.

5 flies are buzzing.

Some more flies join them.

Now there are 8 flies buzzing. $5 + \boxed{} = 8$

Lily has 6 teddy bears.

She finds **some** more.

Now she has 10 teddy bears.   _____

Armand has 8 balloons.

Nora gives him **some** more.

Now he has 12 balloons.    _____

Seven girls are on the bus.

Some more girls get on the bus.

Now **nine** girls are on the bus.   _____

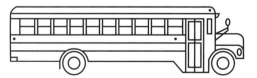

☐ Write the missing numbers.

Addition Problems with an Unknown Start

☐ Find the missing number by counting on.

$5 +$ _____ $= 9$

$6 +$ _____ $= 8$

$6 +$ _____ $= 10$

$8 +$ _____ $= 10$

_____ $+ 2 = 6$

_____ $+ 3 = 4$

$6 +$ _____ $= 9$

_____ $+ 7 = 9$

$16 +$ _____ $= 19$

_____ $+ 17 = 19$

$8 +$ _____ $= 12$

$8 +$ _____ $= 14$

_____ $+ 10 = 15$

_____ $+ 17 = 20$

Bonus

_____ $+ 42 = 46$

Bonus

$96 +$ _____ $= 100$

☐ Write the addition sentence with a box.

Some bees are buzzing.
2 more bees join them.
Now 8 bees are buzzing.

$$\boxed{} + 2 = 8$$

Some girls are on the bus.
3 more girls get on the bus.
Now 9 girls are on the bus.

_____

Avril has **some** marbles.
Jane gives her 5 more.
Now Avril has 12 marbles.

_____

Some bunnies are hopping.
8 more bunnies join them.
Now 13 bunnies are hopping.

_____

Eric has **some** stickers.
He finds **three** more stickers.
Now he has **ten** stickers.

_____

☐ Write the missing numbers.

☐ Write the addition sentence with a box.

3 birds are flying.
Some more join them.
Now 5 birds are flying.

$3 + \boxed{} = 5$

_____

Some fish are swimming.
4 fish join them.
Now 9 fish are swimming.   _____

5 ducks are in a pond.
Some more ducks join them.
Now 8 ducks are in the pond.   _____

Tom has **some** beads.
He gets **six** more.
Now he has **eight** beads.   _____

Three people are dancing.
Nine more join them. Now how
many people are dancing?   _____

☐ Write the missing numbers.

Number Sense 1-93

Parts and Totals

There are red and green apples.

☐ Draw the red apples. Colour them.
☐ Draw the green apples. Do not colour them.
☐ Write how many apples altogether.

2 red apples 3 green apples ● ● ○ ○ ○ ___5___ apples	2 red apples 2 green apples _____ apples
3 red apples 2 green apples _____ apples	2 red apples 1 green apple _____ apples
4 red apples 2 green apples _____ apples	3 red apples 1 green apple _____ apples

There are red and green apples.

☐ Draw all the apples.
☐ Colour the red apples.
☐ How many apples are green?

4 apples in total
3 are red

⬤⬤⬤◯

___1___ green apple

5 apples altogether
4 are red

_____ green apple

there are 3 apples
1 is red

_____ green apples

6 apples in total
2 are red

_____ green apples

there are 5 apples
2 are red

_____ green apples

4 apples altogether
2 are red

_____ green apples

☐ Draw a picture to find the answer.

5 apples in total 3 are red ● ● ● ○ ○ ___2___ green apples	5 red apples 2 green apples _____ apples
4 red apples 3 green apples _____ apples	6 apples altogether 1 is red _____ green apples
8 apples in total 4 are red _____ green apples	1 red apple 4 green apples _____ apples
3 red apples 3 green apples _____ apples	there are 7 apples 2 are red _____ green apples

Addition Sentence Word Problems

☐ Write the addition sentence with a box.
☐ Write the missing number.

There are 5 cars.

3 of them are red.

The rest are blue.

How many are blue?

$3 +$ ☐2 $= 5$

_____

4 apples are red.

5 apples are green.

How many apples in total? _____

There are 6 toys.

4 are cars.

The rest are trucks.

How many are trucks? _____

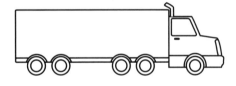

There are **five** children.

There are **two** adults.

How many people in total? _____

☐ Write the addition sentence with a box.
☐ Write the missing number.

There are 7 pets

4 are dogs.

The rest are cats.

How many are cats? _____

There are 10 kites.

4 of them are green.

The rest are red.

How many are red? _____

Kate has 5 hockey cards.

She has 3 baseball cards.

How many cards altogether? _____

There are **ten** children at the park.

There are **three** adults at the park.

How many people in total? _____

Counting On to Subtract

☐ Subtract by counting forwards.

4	5	6	7	8	9

$4 + \boxed{5} = 9$ so $9 - 4 = \boxed{5}$

$6 + \boxed{} = 8$ so $8 - 6 = \boxed{}$

$8 + \boxed{} = 9$ so $9 - 8 = \boxed{}$

$3 + \boxed{} = 8$ so $8 - 3 = \boxed{}$

$7 + \boxed{} = 10$ so $10 - 7 = \boxed{}$

$9 - 5 = \boxed{}$ $10 - 5 = \boxed{}$

$8 - 4 = \boxed{}$ $7 - 2 = \boxed{}$

Number Sense 1-96

Subtraction Problems with an Unknown Change

☐ Fill in the blank. Use the subtraction sentence.

8 − 3 = 5 8 − ___ = 3	9 − 2 = 7 9 − ___ = 2	5 − 2 = 3 5 − ___ = 2
6 − 1 = 5 6 − ___ = 1	8 − 6 = 2 8 − ___ = 6	7 − 3 = 4 7 − ___ = 3

☐ Subtract to find the missing number.

7 − ___ = 4	5 − ___ = 1	6 − ___ = 3
8 − ___ = 4	7 − ___ = 2	10 − ___ = 2

Bonus	**Bonus**
19 − _____ = 9	18 − _____ = 10
Bonus	**Bonus**
83 − _____ = 2	100 − _____ = 4

☐ Write the subtraction sentence with a box.

7 bees are buzzing.
Some bees stop buzzing.
Now 3 bees are buzzing.

$$7 - \boxed{} = 3$$

8 girls are on the bus.
Some girls get off the bus.
Now 6 girls are on the bus. _____

Jin has 10 marbles.
He loses **some** of them.
Now he has 8 marbles. _____

5 boys are standing.
Some boys sit down.
Now 2 boys are standing. _____

Anib has **seven** berries.
She eats **some** of them.
Now she has **four** berries. _____

☐ Write the missing numbers.

☐ Write the number sentence with a box.

7 monkeys are playing.
Some monkeys **join** them.
Now 11 monkeys are playing.

$$7 + \boxed{} = 11$$

8 girls are on the bus.
Some girls **get on** the bus.
Now 10 girls are on the bus. _____

9 people are at the zoo.
Some people **leave**.
Now 6 people are at the zoo. _____

5 boys are standing.
Some **more** boys **stand up**.
Now 8 boys are standing. _____

Eight frogs are jumping.
Some frogs **stop** jumping.
Now **five** frogs are jumping. _____

☐ Write the missing numbers.

Subtraction Problems with an Unknown Start

☐ Fill in the blank. Use the addition sentence.

$3 + 4 = 7$	$3 + 6 = 9$	$5 + 2 = 7$
___ $- 3 = 4$	___ $- 3 = 6$	___ $- 5 = 2$

$2 + 2 = 4$	$4 + 1 = 5$	$1 + 7 = 8$
___ $- 2 = 2$	___ $- 4 = 1$	___ $- 1 = 7$

☐ Add to find the missing number.

___ $- 2 = 4$	___ $- 3 = 1$	___ $- 2 = 2$

___ $- 6 = 4$	___ $- 7 = 7$	___ $- 9 = 9$

___ $- 0 = 5$	___ $- 3 = 12$	___ $- 10 = 7$

Bonus

___ $- 84 = 2$

Bonus

___ $- 3 = 96$

☐ Write the subtraction sentence with a box.

Some flies are buzzing.
2 flies stop buzzing.
Now 8 flies are buzzing.

$\boxed{} - 2 = 8$
_____

Some girls are on the bus.
3 girls get off the bus.
Now 6 girls are on the bus.
_____

Alex has **some** balloons.
He loses 5 of them.
Now he has 7 balloons.
_____

Tasha has **some** berries.
Then she eats **four** of them.
Now she has **nine** berries.
_____

Bonus

Ben has **some** apples.
He gives 2 to Ed and 3 to Iva.
Now Ben has 4 apples.
_____

☐ Write the missing numbers.

☐ Write the number sentence with a box.

Some ducks are quacking.
4 ducks **stop** quacking.
Now 5 ducks are quacking.

$\boxed{} - 4 = 5$

Some girls are on the bus.
7 girls **get off** the bus.
Now 3 girls are on the bus.

_____

Jen has some stickers.
She **loses** 2 of them.
Now she has 12 stickers.

_____

Some boys are on the bus.
8 more boys **get on** the bus.
Now 11 boys are on the bus.

_____

Ethan sees some ants.
He **sees one more**.
Now he sees **eight** ants.

_____

☐ Write the missing numbers.

☐ Write the number sentence with a box.

Some ducks are quacking.
3 ducks **join** them.
Now 5 ducks are quacking. _____

8 girls are on the bus.
Some girls **get off** the bus.
Now 2 girls are on the bus. _____

Hanna has 7 beads.
She **loses** 2 of them.
Now she has **some** beads. _____

Some boys are on the bus.
3 boys **get off** the bus.
Now 11 boys are on the bus. _____

Braden has **six** flowers.
He finds **some** more.
Now he has **eight** flowers. _____

☐ Write the missing numbers.

Subtraction and How Many More

☐ Use how many more to subtract.

6 is 2 more than 4. 6 − 4 = ___	7 is 5 more than 2. 7 − 2 = ___

☐ Subtract to find how many more.

10 − 1 = ___ 10 is ___ more than 1.	8 − 2 = ___ 8 is ___ more than 2.
9 − 4 = ___ 9 is ___ more than 4.	15 − 2 = ___ 15 is ___ more than 2.

☐ How many more beavers than deer?

There are 7 beavers and 5 deer. _____

There are 8 beavers and 3 deer. _____

There are 12 beavers and 4 deer. _____

☐ Add or subtract to answer the question.

Aki has 8 stickers. Ken has 3 stickers.
How many more stickers does Aki have?

_____

Lela has 7 toy trucks. Jake has 2 more toy
trucks than Lela. How many does Jake have?

_____

There are 4 whales and 6 seals.
How many more seals than whales?

_____

Ella is six years old. Marcel is three years
older than Ella. How old is Marcel?

_____

Bonus

Raj sees 3 bears and 7 deer. He sees 1 more
bear. How many more deer than bears?

_____

Mixed Word Problems

☐ Solve the problem.

There are 3 big bears and 2 small bears. How many bears altogether?

_____

Some children go to the park. 3 more join them. Now there are 8 children at the park. How many were at the park at first?

_____

7 children and 4 adults are at the park. How many more children than adults?

_____

There are 20 beavers. 18 of them are small. How many are big?

_____

12 moose are eating. Some moose stop eating. Now 6 moose are eating. How many moose stopped eating?

_____

☐ Solve the problem.

David has 5 red marbles and 6 green marbles.
He gives some to Ava. Now David has 8 marbles.
How many did he give to Ava?

Jeri has 10 nickels. She gives 4 to Ed and
3 to Jack. She keeps the rest. Who has
the most nickels now, Jeri, Ed, or Jack?

There are 20 people at the beach.
7 are adults. Are there more children
or adults? How many more?

Patterns in the Hundreds Chart

☐ Circle the ones digit in each shaded square.

1	2	3	4	5	6	7	8	9	10
11	12	13	14	15	16	17	18	19	20
21	22	23	24	25	26	27	28	29	30

☐ Write the **ones digit** from each **shaded** square.

__2__, __4__, __6__, __8__, __0__,

__2__, __4__, ____, ____, ____,

____, ____, ____, ____, ____

☐ Write the next 5 ones digits.

____, ____, ____, ____, ____

☐ Write the **ones digit** from each **white** square.

__1__, __3__, __5__, __7__, __9__,

__1__, __3__, ____, ____, ____,

____, ____, ____, ____, ____

☐ Write the next 5 ones digits.

____, ____, ____, ____, ____

☐ Write the **ones digit** from each shaded square.

_____, _____, _____, _____, _____,

_____, _____, _____, _____, _____

1	2	3
11	12	13
21	22	23
31	32	33
41	42	43
51	52	53
61	62	63
71	72	73
81	82	83
91	92	93

☐ Describe the pattern.

_____

_____

_____

_____

☐ Shade the counting by 5s numbers.

1	2	3	4	5	6	7	8	9	10
11	12	13	14	15	16	17	18	19	20
21	22	23	24	25	26	27	28	29	30

☐ Write the ones digit from each shaded square.

_____, _____, _____, _____, _____, _____

☐ Describe the pattern. _____

☐ Write the next 4 ones digits.

_____, _____, _____, _____

Equal and Not Equal

☐ Write the number of cubes on each side.
☐ Write = or ≠ in the box.

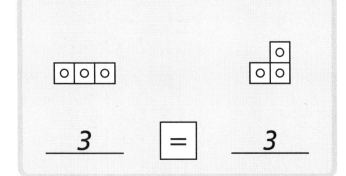

___3___ = ___3___

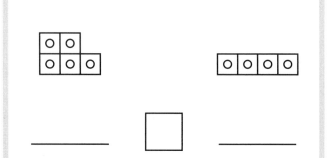

_____ ☐ _____

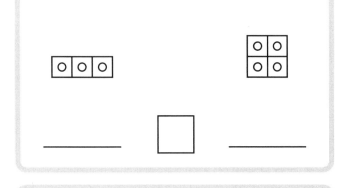

_____ ☐ _____

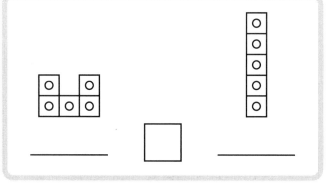

_____ ☐ _____

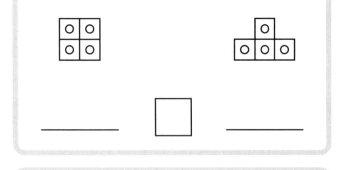

_____ ☐ _____

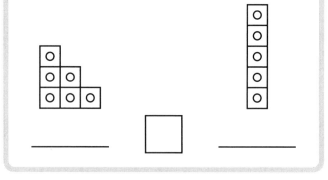

_____ ☐ _____

Patterns and Algebra 1-9

☐ Write the addition sentence.

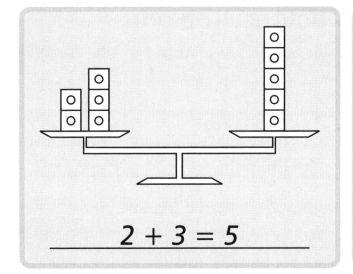

$2 + 3 = 5$

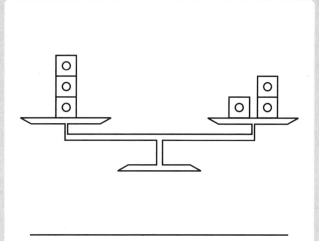

_____

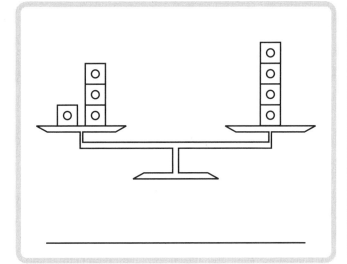

_____

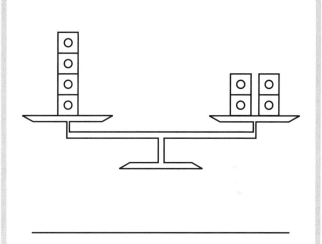

_____

Bonus

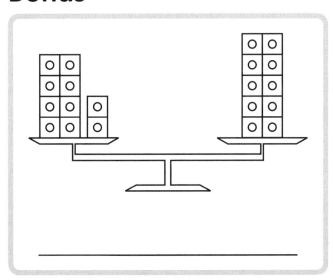

_____

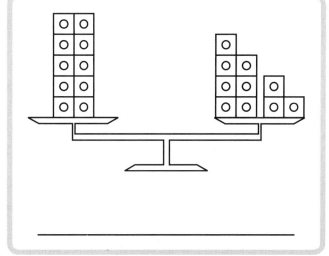

_____

Balances and Missing Numbers

☐ Add cubes to one side to balance the pans.

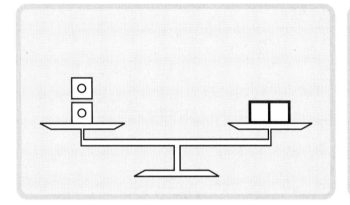

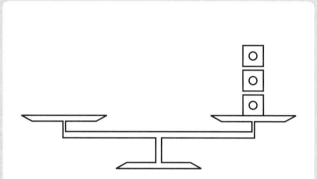

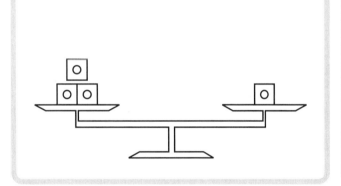

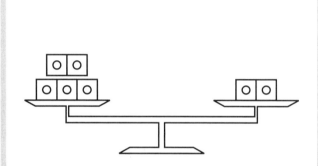

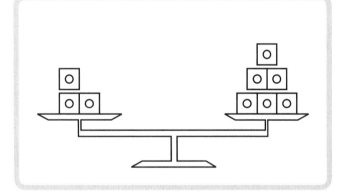

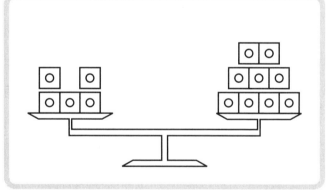

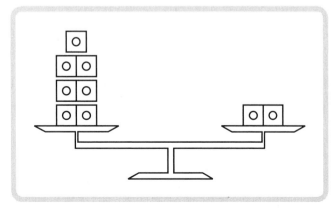

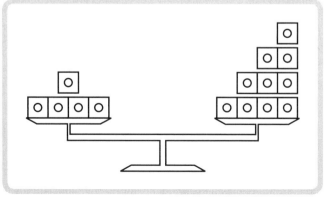

☐ Add balls to one side to balance the pans.
☐ Write an addition sentence.

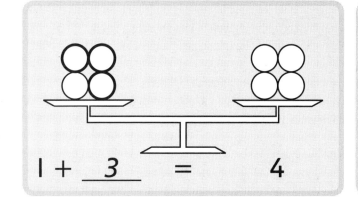

1 + _3_ = 4

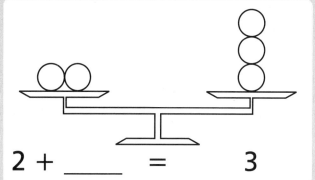

2 + ____ = 3

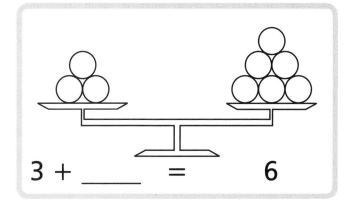

3 + ____ = 6

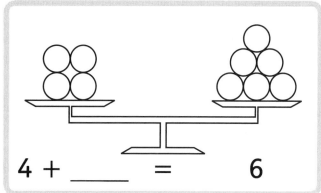

4 + ____ = 6

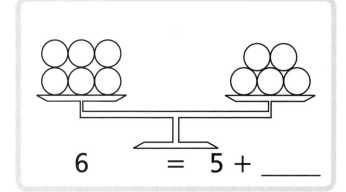

6 = 5 + ____

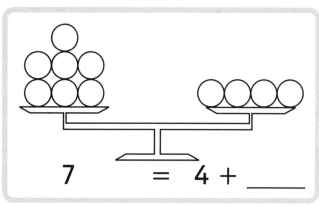

7 = 4 + ____

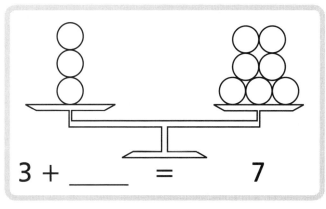

3 + ____ = 7

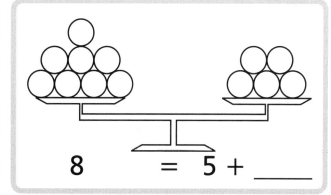

8 = 5 + ____

Remove cubes from one side to balance the pans.

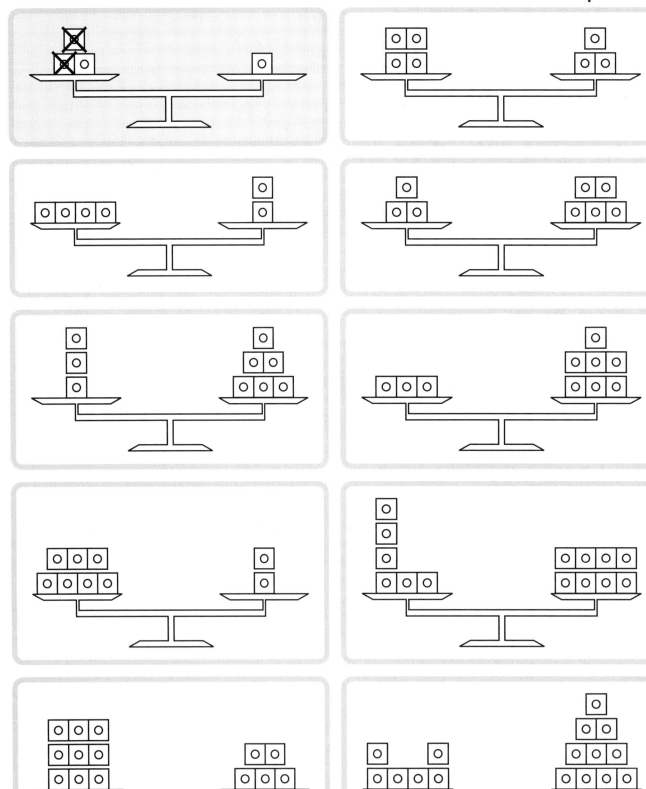

Remove fruit from one side to balance the pans.
Write a subtraction sentence.

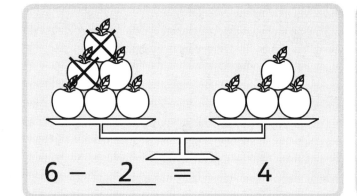

6 − __2__ = 4

5 − ____ = 1

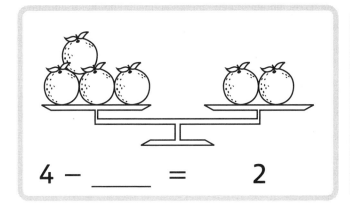

4 − ____ = 2

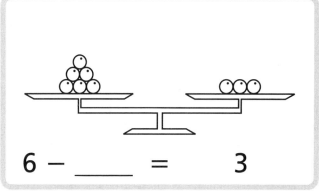

6 − ____ = 3

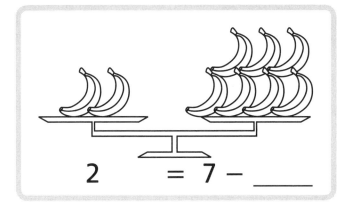

2 = 7 − ____

4 = 8 − ____

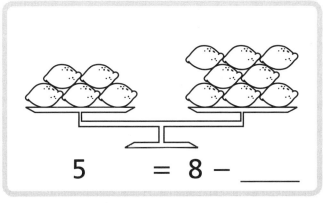

5 = 8 − ____

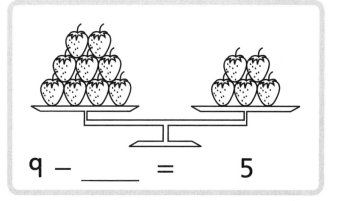

9 − ____ = 5

Location Words

☐ Write **above** or **below**.

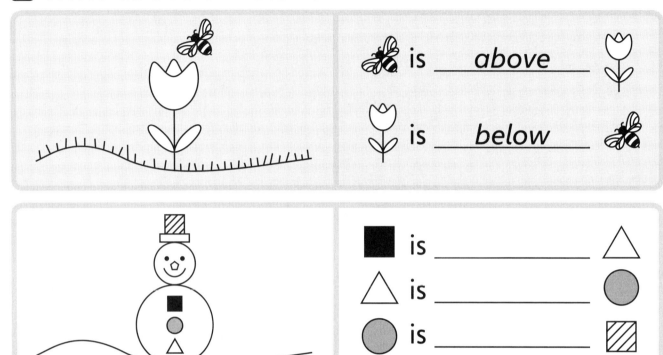

☐ Circle the people **beside** 😊.

 is **between** and .

☐ Circle the people **between** and .

Bonus: Colour the rows between the shaded rows.

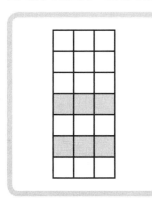

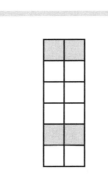

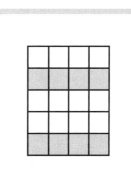

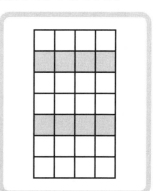

_____2_____ people are in front of .

_____ people are behind .

_____ people are in front of .

_____ people are behind .

_____ people are in front of .

_____ people are behind .

☐ Write **in front of** or **behind**.

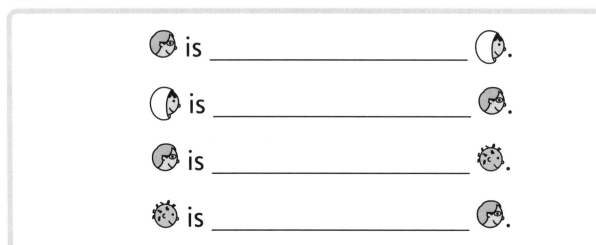

More Location Words

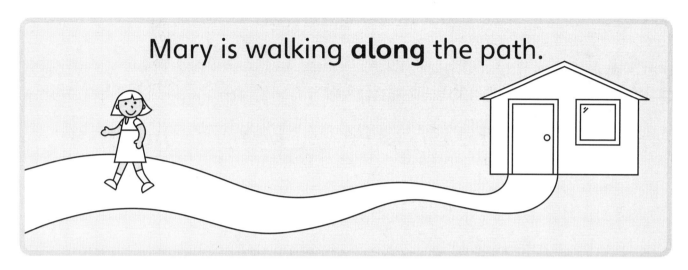

Mary is walking **along** the path.

☐ Circle the people walking **along** the path.

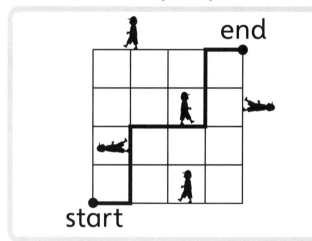

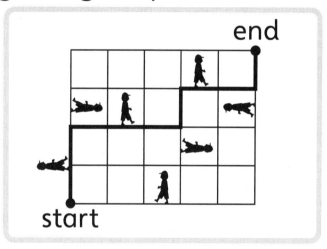

☐ Trace any path from **start** to **end**.
☐ Circle the people walking along your path.

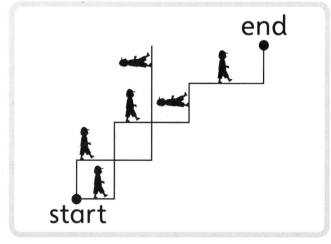

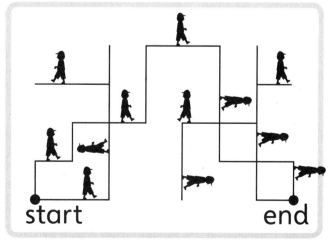

☐ Write **over** or **under**.

The cow jumped _____*over*_____ the moon.
The pig flew _____*under*_____ the moon.

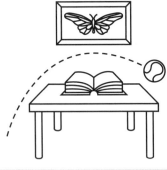
The plane flew _____ the clouds.
The bird flew _____ the clouds.

☐ Write **over**, **above**, or **on top of**.

The picture is _____ the table.
The book is _____ the table.
The ball goes _____ the table.

The car drove _____ the hill.
The tree is _____ the hill.
The moon is _____ the hill.

☐ Write **inside** or **outside**.

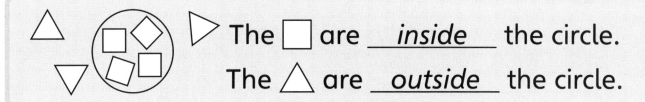 The ☐ are ___*inside*___ the circle.
The △ are ___*outside*___ the circle.

 The ♡ is _____ the square.
The ◯ is _____ the square.

 The ⊶⬤⬤⬤⊷ are _____ the bowl.
The ◯ are _____ the bowl.

 is _____ the house.
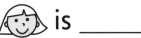 is _____ the house.

 The ◯ is _____ the rectangle.
The ◯ is _____ the triangle.

Bonus: Fill in the blanks.

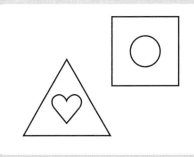 The ◯ is _____ the triangle.
The ♡ is inside the _____.
The _____ is inside the square.

Symmetry

parts match **exactly**	parts **do not** match

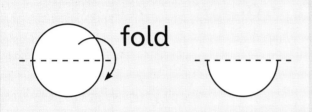 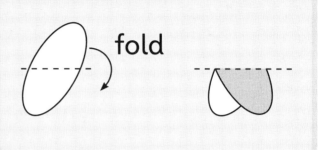

☐ Do the parts match exactly? Write **yes** or **no**.

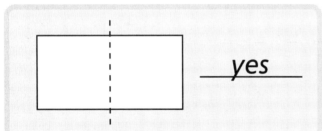

yes

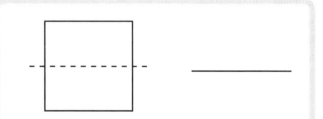

_____

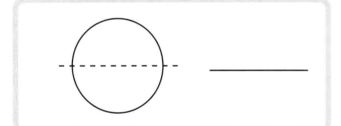

_____

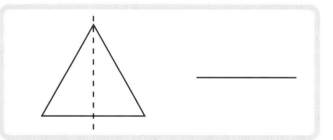

_____

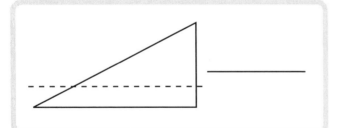

_____

_____

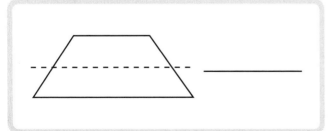

_____

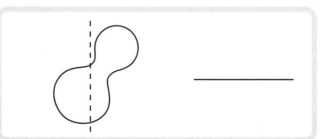

_____

Geometry 1-14

☐ Draw a line to show the symmetry.

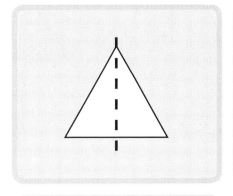  

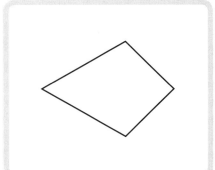 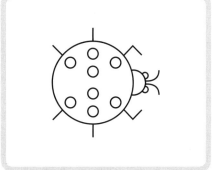 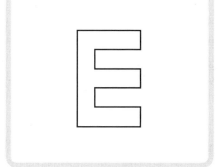

☐ Does the shape have symmetry?

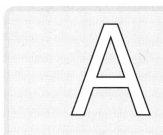

yes

___

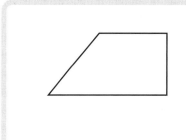

___

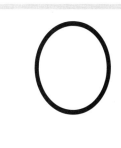

___

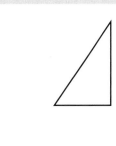

___

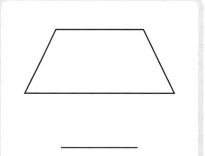

___

Bonus: Draw the lines that show symmetry.

☐ Finish the shape. Use symmetry.

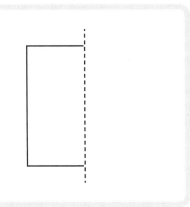
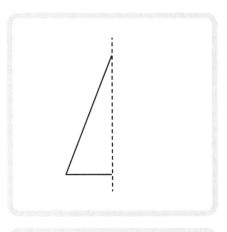

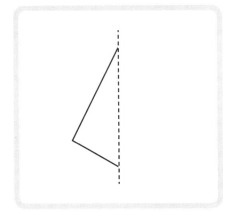
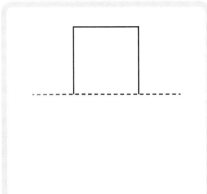
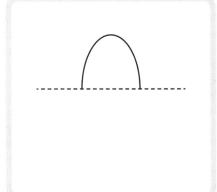

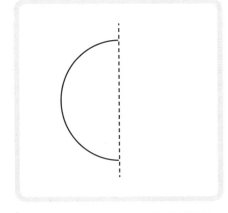
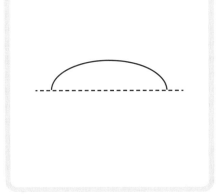
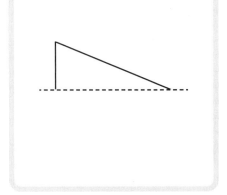

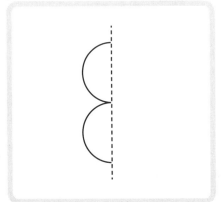
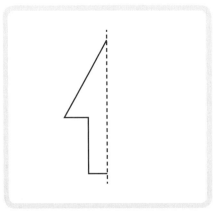

Bonus:

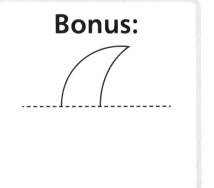

Cubes and Rectangular Prisms

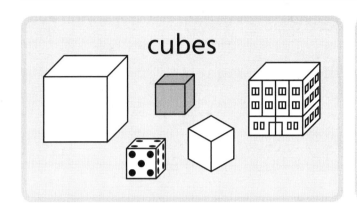

cubes

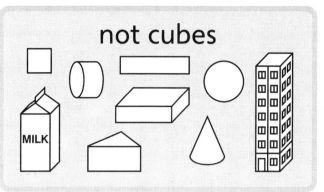

not cubes

☐ Circle the objects that look like cubes.

 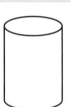 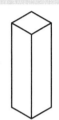

    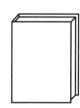

☐ Draw 2 more objects that are almost cubes.

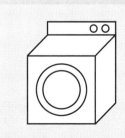  

rectangular prisms	not rectangular prisms
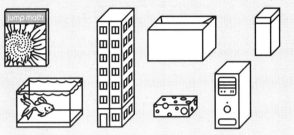	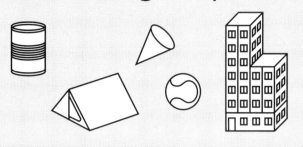

☐ Circle the objects that look like rectangular prisms.

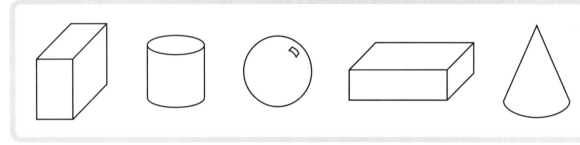

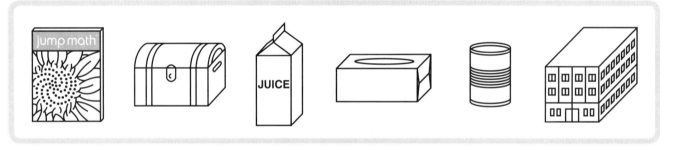

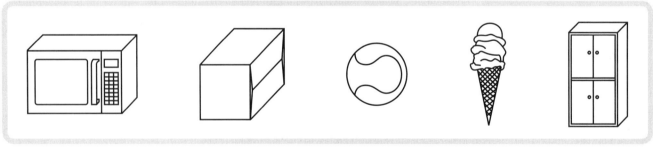

☐ Draw objects that look like rectangular prisms.

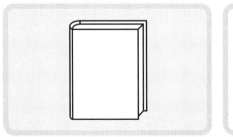  

Spheres, Cylinders, and Cones

spheres	not spheres
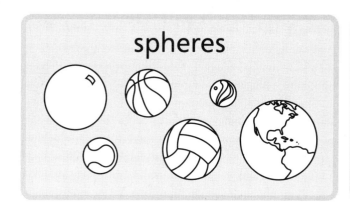	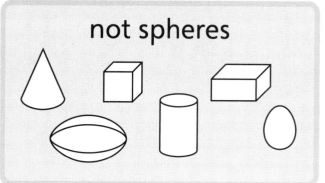

☐ Circle the objects that look like spheres.

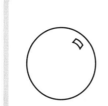

☐ Draw 2 more objects that are almost spheres.

cylinders	not cylinders
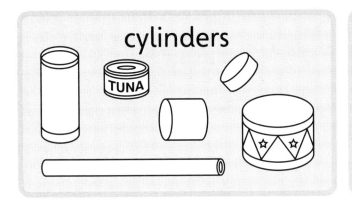	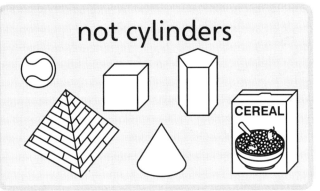

☐ Circle the objects that look like cylinders.

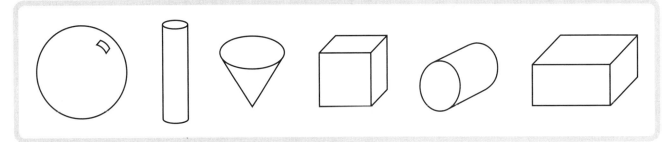

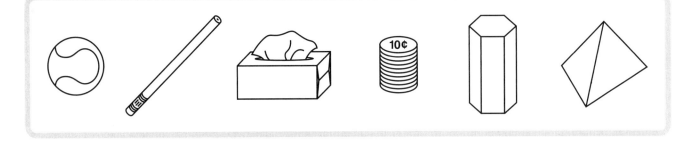

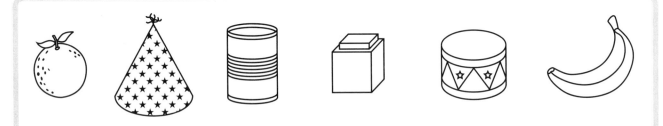

☐ Draw 2 more objects that are almost cylinders.

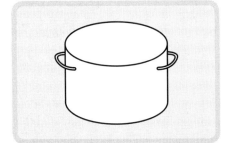  

cones	not cones
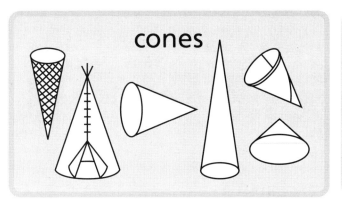	

☐ Circle the objects that look like cones.

☐ Draw 2 more objects that are almost cones.

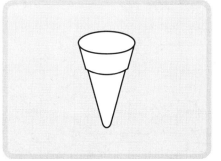  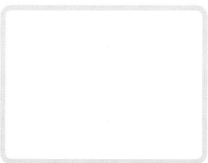

Flat and Curved Faces

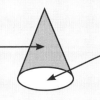

Curved faces roll. **Flat faces** slide.

☐ Colour the **curved faces** orange.
☐ Colour the **flat faces** blue.

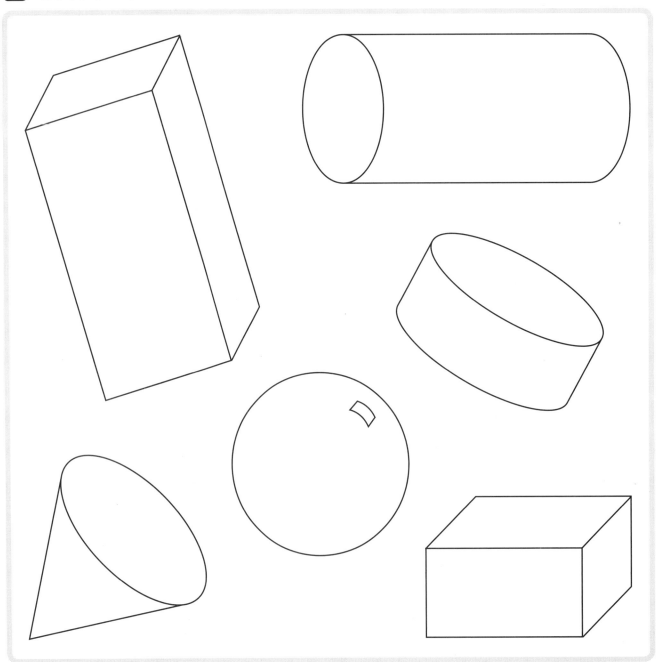

☐ Sort.

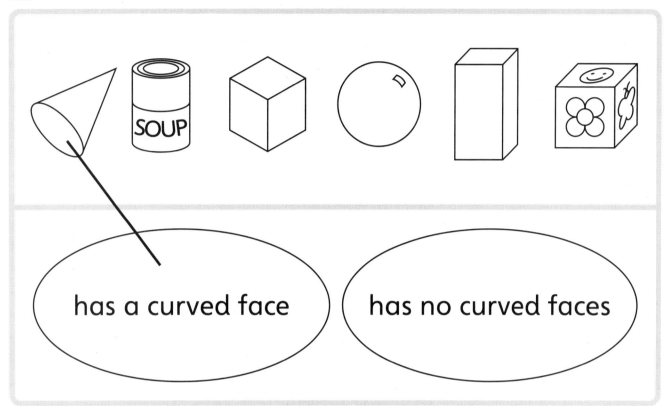

☐ Now sort another way.

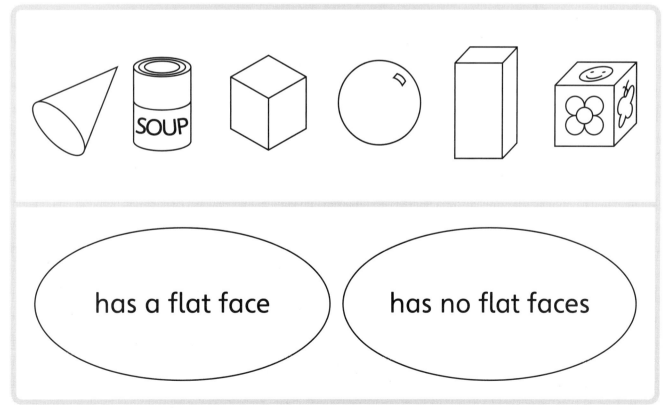

Identifying 3-D Shapes

☐ What is the shape of the shaded face? Circle it.

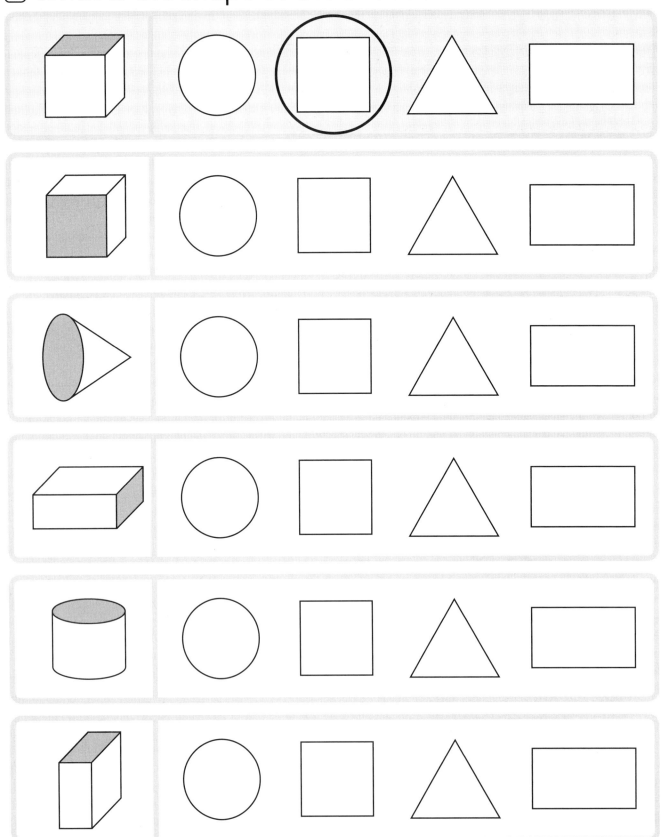

☐ Sort.

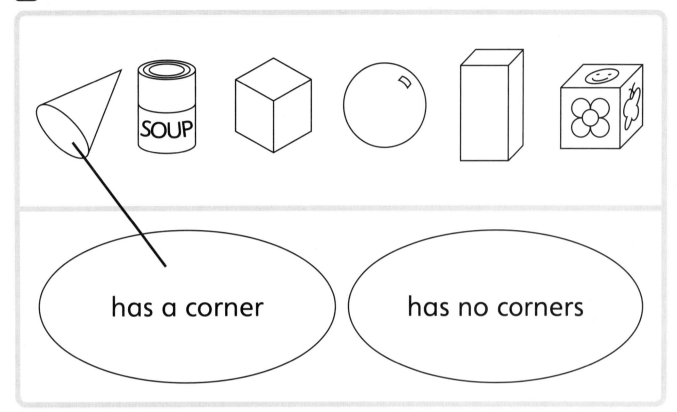

has a corner   has no corners

☐ Now sort your way.

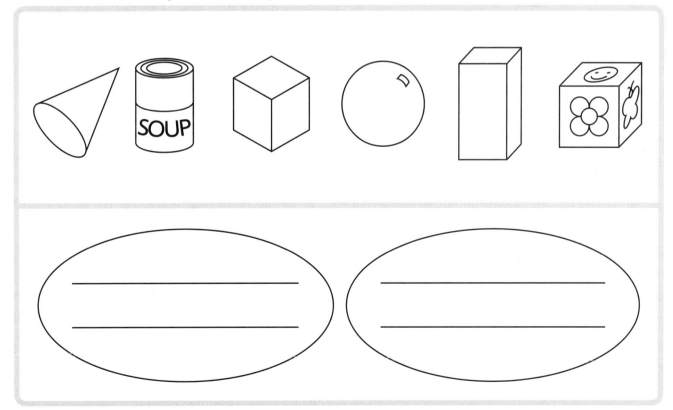

| cone | cube | cylinder | prism | sphere |

☐ Circle the correct shape. Write its name.

I have 6 faces.

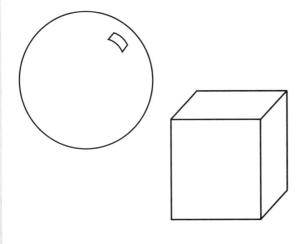

I am a _____.

I have a curved face.

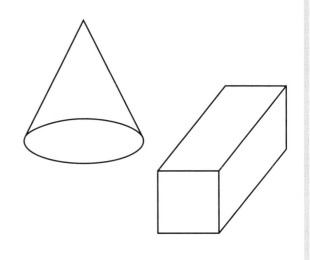

I am a _____.

I have 2 flat faces.

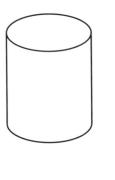 

I am a _____.

I roll.

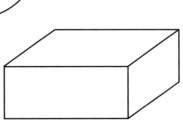

I am a _____.

Composing 3-D Shapes

Colour.

yellow

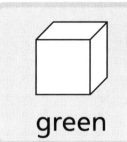
green

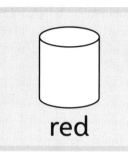
red

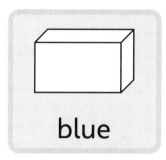
blue

Mandy makes a building from blocks.

☐ Circle the shapes she uses.

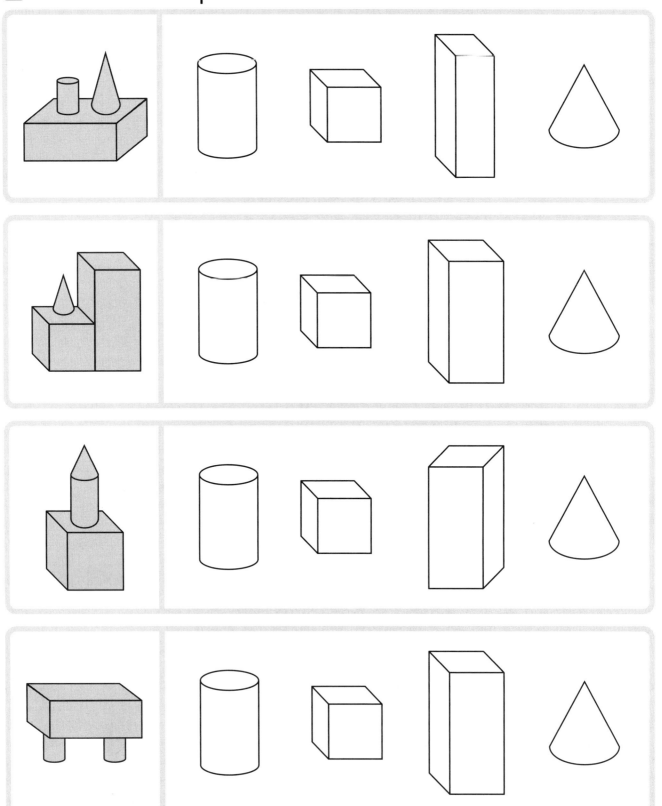

| cone | cube | cylinder | prism | sphere |

☐ Write the name beside the shape.
☐ Fill in the blank.

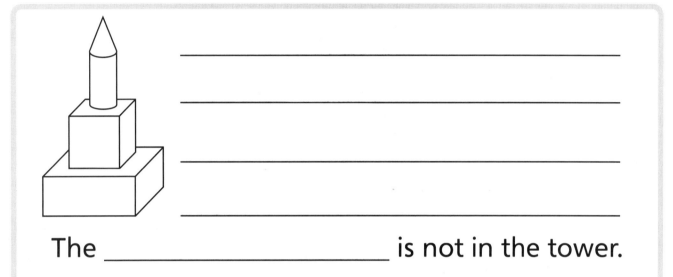

_____

_____

_____

_____

The _____ is not in the tower.

☐ Write how many.

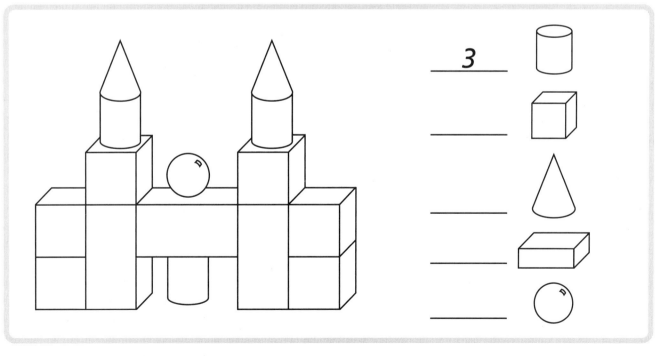

__3__

_____

_____

_____

_____

Bonus: Build the castle.

Maps

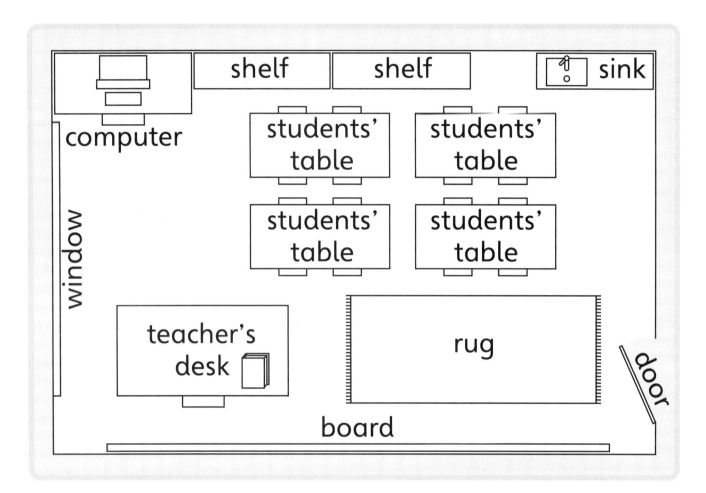

☐ Write **beside**, **between**, or **on top of**.

The computer is _____ the shelf.

The book is _____ the teacher's desk.

The rug is _____ the students' tables and the board.

The shelves are _____ the sink.

The shelves are _____ the computer and the sink.

Clock Faces

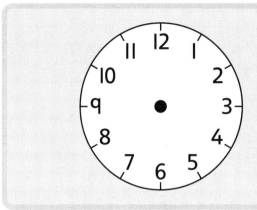

This is a clock face.

Numbers start at 1
and end at 12.

☐ Fill in the missing 3, 6, 9, or 12.

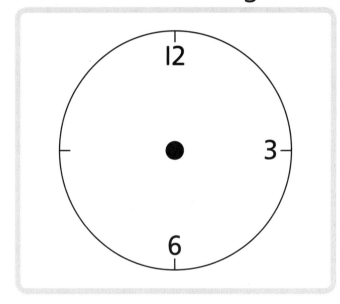

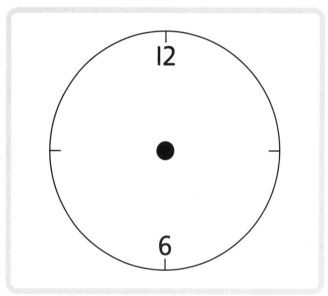

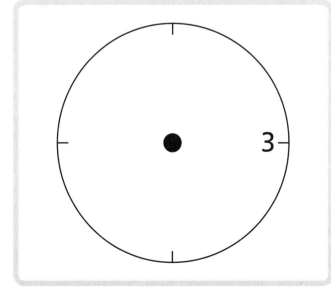

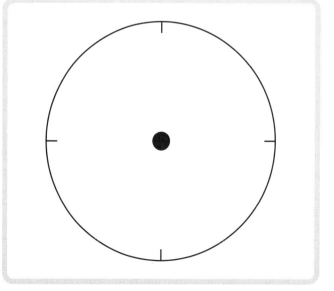

☐ Fill in the missing numbers.

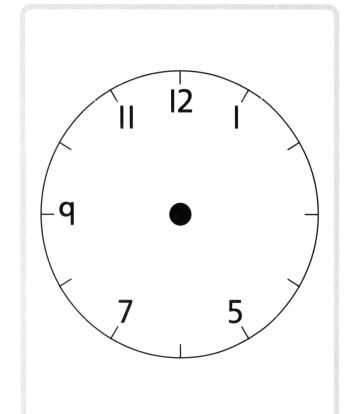

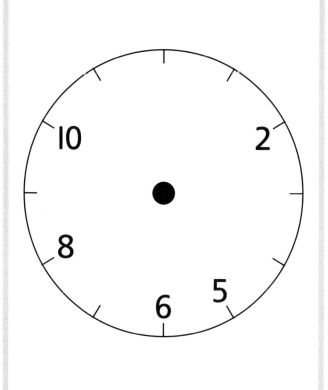

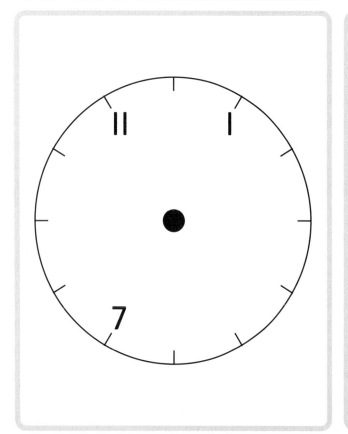

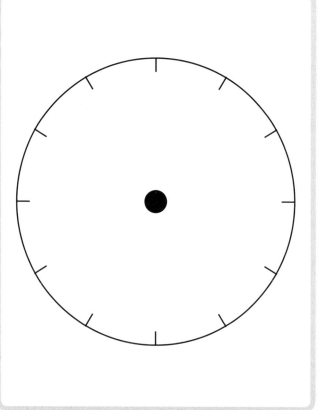

Comparing Times

☐ Sing the alphabet when your partner starts.
How far do you get when your partner ...

does 5 jumping jacks?  ___	spins around?  ___
traces these shapes? 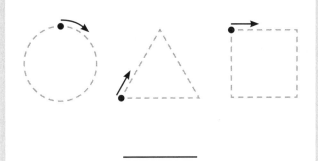 ___	stands up and sits down?  ___
writes "hello"? ___	erases "hello"?  ___

What took the longest time? _____

What took the shortest time? _____

Using Clocks to Measure Time

☐ Start when the fast hand is at the 12.
Where is the fast hand when you finish?

Trace your hand.
Use a pencil.

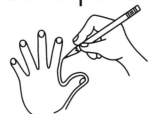
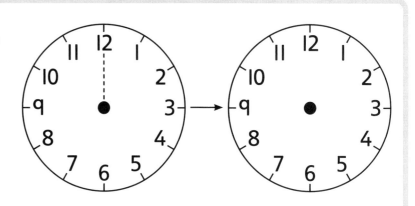

Colour your picture.
Use a pencil.

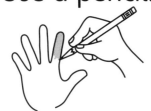
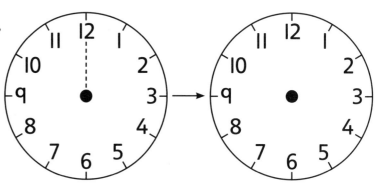

Erase your picture.

Tracing / Colouring / Erasing took the shortest time.

Tracing / Colouring / Erasing took the longest time.

Amir is juggling.
How many steps did the fast hand take?

starts   stops   ___3___

starts   stops   _____

starts   stops   _____

Bonus

_____   _____   _____

The Hour Hand

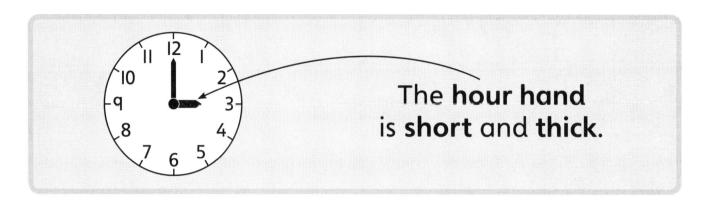

The **hour hand** is **short** and **thick**.

☐ Circle the hour hand.

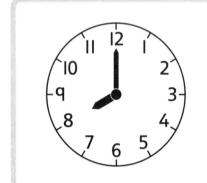

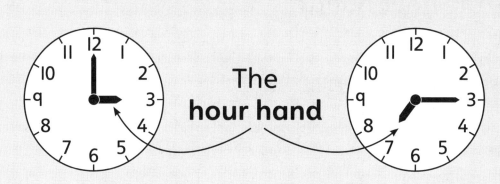

The **hour hand**

The hour hand is pointing **at the 3**.

The hour hand is pointing **close to the 7**.

Where is the hour hand pointing?

at the ___

close to the ___

at the ___

close to the ___

at the ___

at the ___

Where is the hour hand?

school starts
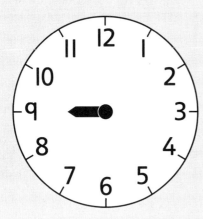

recess starts
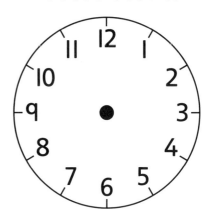

recess finishes
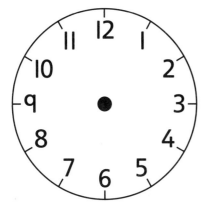

lunch starts
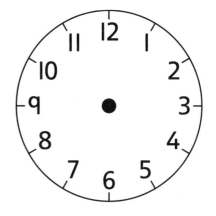

lunch finishes
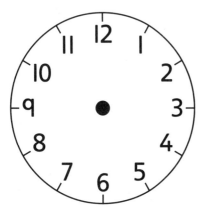

school finishes
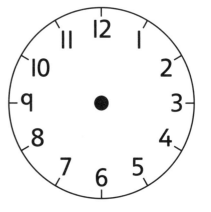

How long does the party last?

starts	ends	

_____ o'clock	_____ o'clock	_____ hours

starts	ends	

_____ o'clock	_____ o'clock	_____ hours

starts	ends	

_____ o'clock	_____ o'clock	_____ hours

starts	ends	

_____ o'clock	_____ o'clock	_____ hours

Time to the Hour

 It is **9** o'clock.

☐ Write the time shown on the clock.

_____ o'clock

_____ o'clock

_____ o'clock

_____

_____

_____

_____

_____

_____

☐ Write the time in two ways.

___6___ o'clock

___6___ :00

_____ o'clock

_____ :00

_____ o'clock

_____ :00

_____

_____ : _____

_____

_____ : _____

_____

_____ : _____

_____

_____

_____

_____

_____

_____

☐ Draw the hands. Draw the hour hand shorter.

3:00	2 o'clock	5:00
		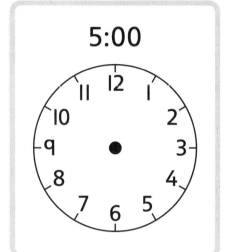
11 o'clock	7:00	12 o'clock
	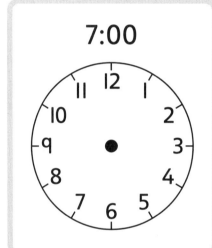	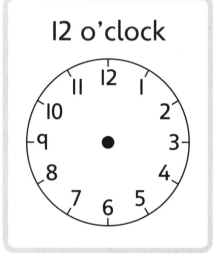
7 o'clock	6 o'clock	9:00
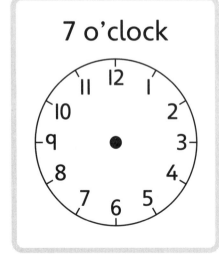		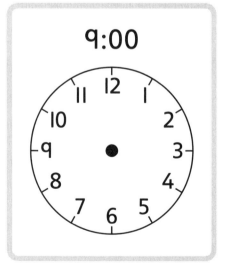

Bonus: Circle the clocks that are the same.

You play for **1 hour**. What time will you finish?

start at   finish at

8:00   9:00

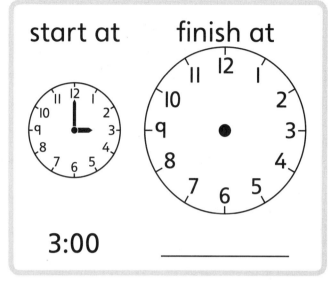

start at   finish at

3:00   _____

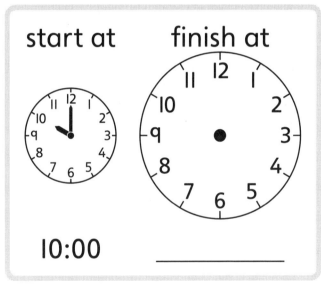

start at   finish at

10:00   _____

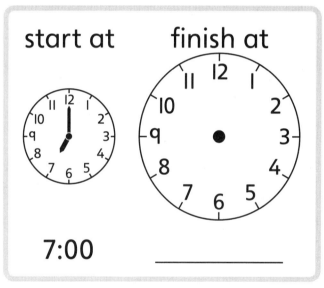

start at   finish at

7:00   _____

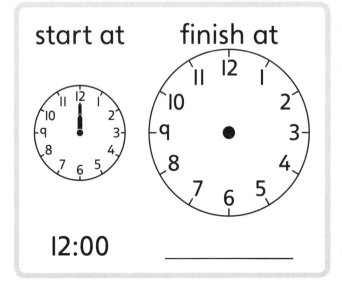

start at   finish at

12:00   _____

start at   finish at

11:00   _____

The lesson starts at **4:00**.

It lasts for **1 hour**.

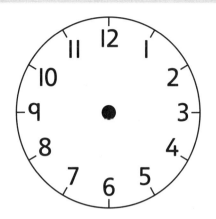

It ends at _____.

Dad starts cooking at **5:00**.

Dad cooks for **1 hour**.

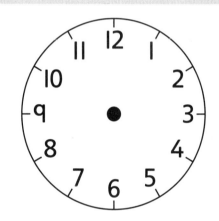

He finishes at _____.

The show starts at **11:00**.

It lasts for **1 hour**.

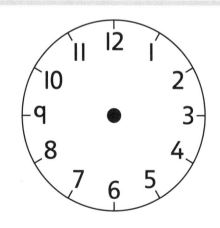

It ends at _____.

Measurement I-23

Time to the Half Hour (I)

 It is **half past 3**.

☐ Write the time.

half past _____

half past _____

half past _____

_____

_____

_____

_____

_____

_____

☐ Write the time in two ways.

half past __3__

__3__ :30

half past _____

_____ :30

half past _____

_____ :30

_____

_____ : _____

_____

_____ : _____

_____

_____ : _____

_____

_____

_____

_____

_____

_____

☐ Draw the hands. Draw the hour hand shorter.

12:30	2:30	4:30
	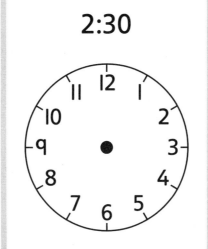	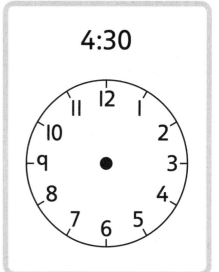

3:30	10:30	8:30
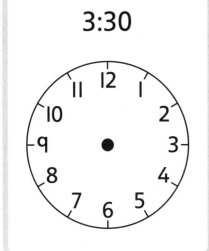	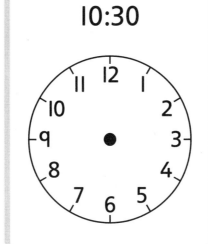	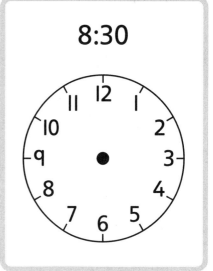

7:30	1:30	6:30
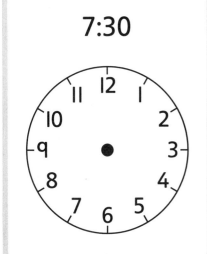	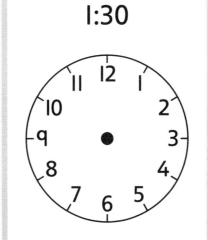	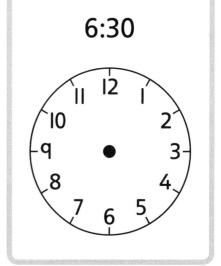

☐ Match the analog times to the digital times.

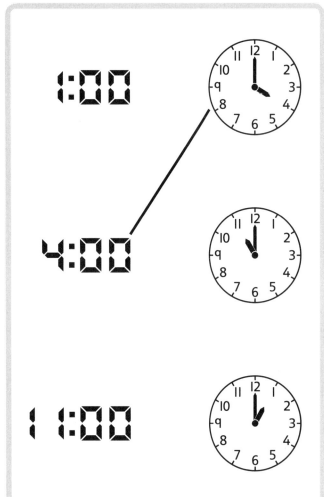

Time to the Half Hour (2)

You swim for **I hour**. What time will you finish?

start at

8:30

finish at

9:30

start at

12:30

finish at

_____

start at

2:30

finish at

_____

start at

4:30

finish at

_____

start at

6:30

finish at

_____

start at

5:30

finish at

_____

Rani starts playing soccer at **4:30**.

She plays for **1 hour**.

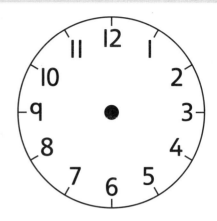

She stops at _____.

Alex starts swimming at **8:30**.

He swims for **1 hour**.

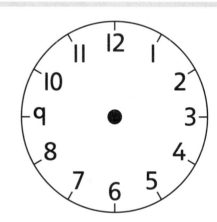

He stops at _____.

We watch TV for **1 hour**.

We start at **6:30**.

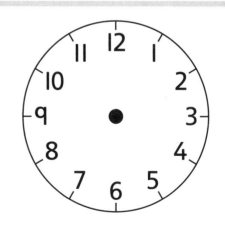

We stop at _____.

Will Jake be finished by 6 o'clock ?

☐ Write **yes** or **no**.

It is **5:00**.

He walks for **1 hour**.

_____yes_____

He plays soccer at **4:00**.

He plays for **2 hours**.

_____

He starts cooking at **4:30**.

He cooks for **1 hour**.

_____

He rides his bike at **4:30**.

He rides for **2 hours**.

_____

Days, Months, and Seasons

☐ Write the days of the week in order.
☐ Circle the days you go to school.

Friday	1. ___*Sunday*___
Thursday	2. _____
Monday	3. _____
Saturday	4. _____
Wednesday	5. _____
~~Sunday~~	6. _____
Tuesday	7. _____

☐ Unscramble the days.

ridFya	_F_ _r_ _i_ _d_ _a_ _y_
Mdoany	___ ___ ___ _d_ _a_ _y_
uSadny	___ ___ ___ ___ ___ ___
uTedsay	___ ___ ___ ___ ___ ___ ___

What day comes after?

Monday	_____
Saturday	_____

☐ Write the months of the year in order.
☐ Circle the months you go to school.

May	1. _____January_____
July	2. _____
December	3. _____
~~January~~	4. _____
March	5. _____
November	6. _____
September	7. _____
June	8. _____
February	9. _____
October	10. _____
August	11. _____
April	12. _____

☐ Unscramble the months.

yaM	____ ____ ____
eJun	____ ____ ____ ____
lyJu	____ ____ ____ ____

Bonus: ybrFeuar ___ ___ ___ ___ ___ ___ ___ ___

In what season can you do this outside?
☐ Write **spring**, **summer**, **fall** or **winter**.

_____

_____

_____

_____

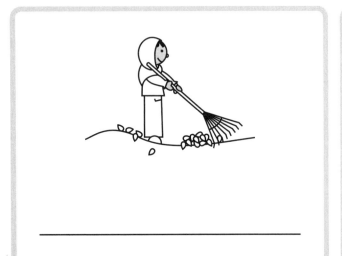

_____

_____

June

Sunday	Monday	Tuesday	Wednesday	Thursday	Friday	Saturday
					1	2
3	4	5	6	7	8	9
10	11	12	13	14	15	16
17	18	19	20	21	22	23
24	25	26	27	28	29	30

What **day** is it?

June 1st _____ *Friday* _____

June 16th _____

June 25th _____

What **date** is it?

the first Wednesday _____ *June 6th* _____

the third Saturday _____

the second Monday _____

Today is **Tuesday, March 6th**.

March

Sunday	Monday	Tuesday	Wednesday	Thursday	Friday	Saturday
				1	2	3
4	5	6	7	8	9	10
11	12	13	14	15	16	17
18	19	20	21	22	23	24
25	26	27	28	29	30	31

What **day** was it yesterday? _____

What **date** will it be tomorrow? _____

Aki has a play date on March 15th.

How many **days** until her play date? _____

Ben's birthday is in exactly 1 week.

What **day** is his birthday? _____

What **date** is his birthday? _____

Comparing Areas

☐ Trace the shapes.
☐ Cut them out and compare the areas.
☐ Write **bigger** or **smaller** on the shapes.

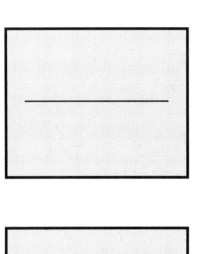

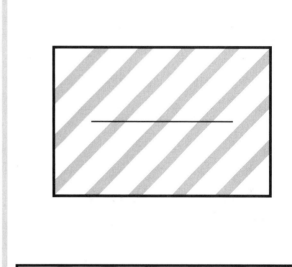

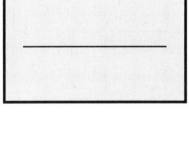

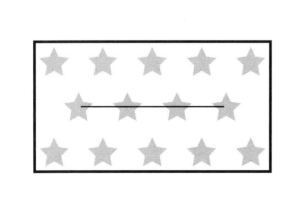

Measuring Areas

Use big 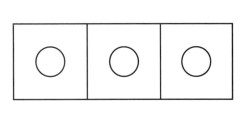 as a unit.

☐ Measure the area.

_____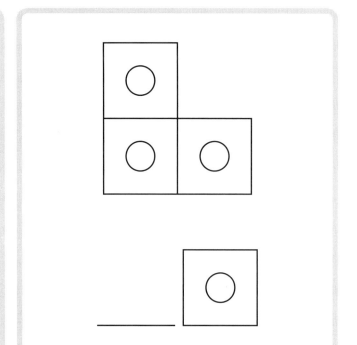

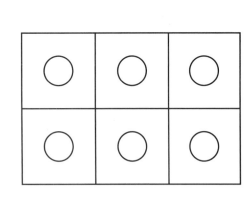

_____

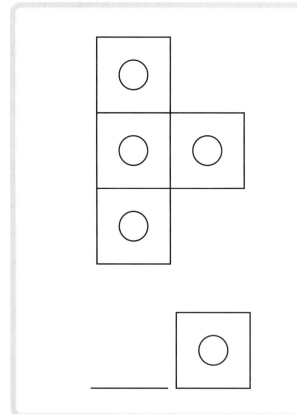

Use big 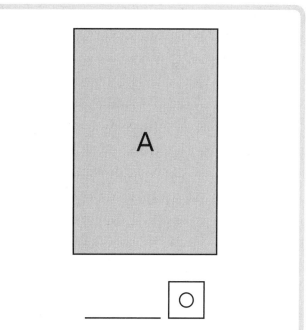 as a unit.

☐ Measure the area.

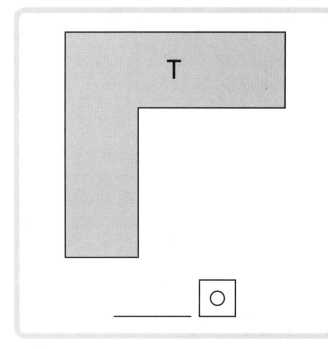

T

_____ ⬚

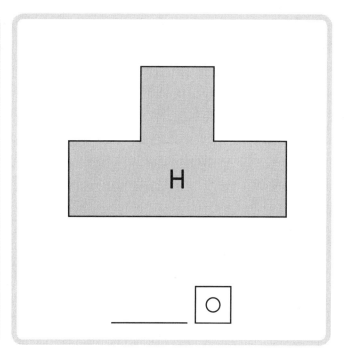

H

_____ ⬚

M

_____ ⬚

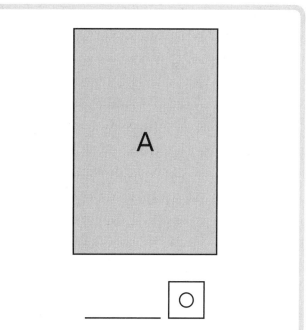

A

_____ ⬚

☐ Order the shapes from biggest to smallest.

_____ _____ _____ _____

☐ Estimate the area.
☐ Check how many big 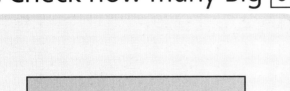.

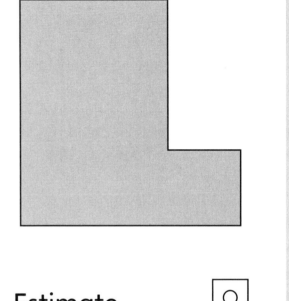

Estimate ___5___ ○

Measure ___4___ ○

Estimate _____ ○

Measure _____ ○

Estimate _____ ○

Measure _____ ○

Use an index card ▤ as a unit.

☐ Estimate the area.
☐ Measure the area.

	Estimate	Measure
(table)	_____ ▤	_____ ▤
(book)	_____ ▤	_____ ▤
(chair)	_____ ▤	_____ ▤
You choose:	_____ ▤	_____ ▤

COPYRIGHT © 2017 JUMP MATH: NOT TO BE COPIED

What Holds More?

☐ Write **less than**, **more than**, or **the same as**.

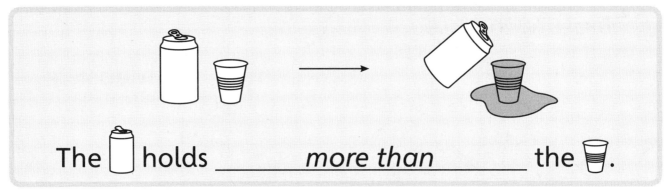

The 🥫 holds _____*more than*_____ the 🥤.

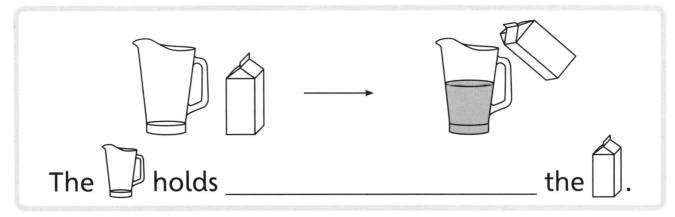

The 🫗 holds _____ the 🥛.

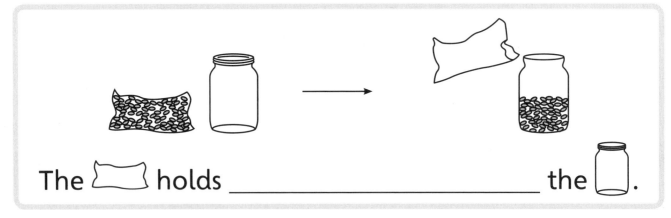

The 🫘 holds _____ the 🫙.

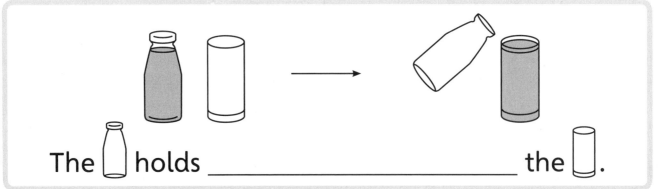

The 🍶 holds _____ the 🥛.

Capacity

☐ Write **less than**, **more than**, or **the same as**.

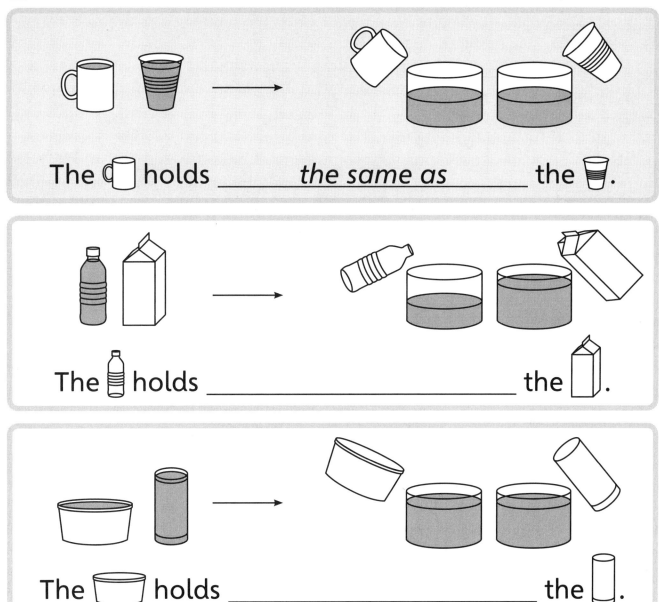

The 🍵 holds _____*the same as*_____ the 🥤.

The 🍶 holds _____ the 🥛.

The 🥣 holds _____ the 🥤.

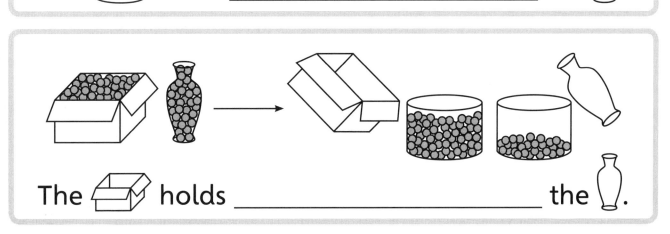

The 📦 holds _____ the 🏺.

Measuring Capacity

☐ Circle the one that holds **more**.

☐ Circle the one that holds **less**.

☐ Circle the one that holds the **most**.

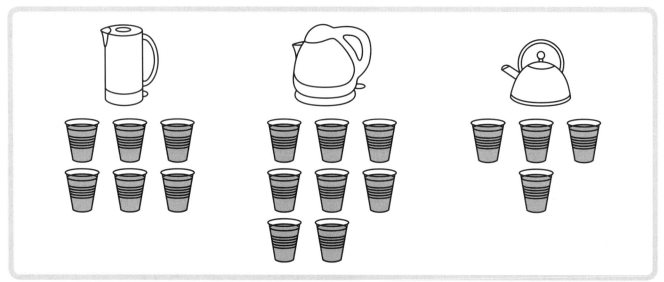

Sorting and Graphing

☐ Sort the objects.
☐ Write the objects in the correct rows.

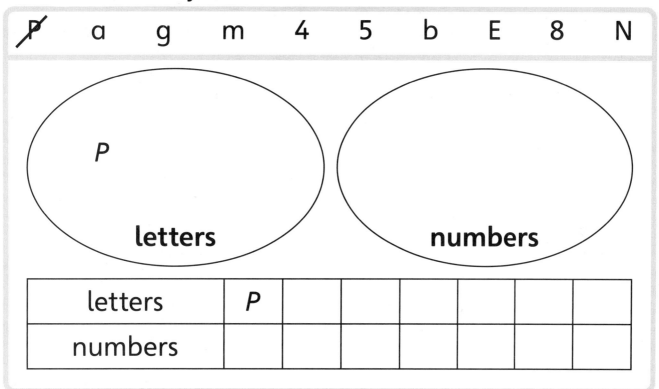

P̸   a   g   m   4   5   b   E   8   N

letters	P						
numbers							

in   red   man   no   yes   at   of

3 letters				
2 letters				

Pictographs

Lunch Time

at home	�	�	�	�	�	�
at school	�	�	�	�		

_6_ eat at home.

_4_ eat at school.

More students eat lunch _____ _at home_ _____.

Mitts or Gloves

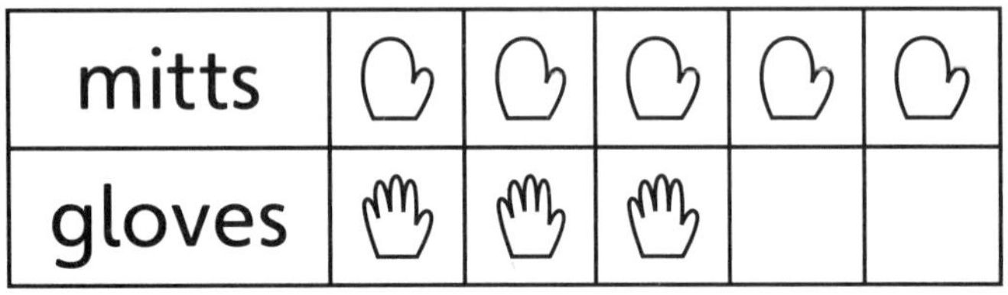

mitts	🧤	🧤	🧤	🧤	🧤
gloves	✋	✋	✋		

_____ wear mitts.

_____ wear gloves.

More students wear _____.

Marko's Garden

tulips	🌷	🌷	🌷	🌷	🌷
roses	🌀	🌀	🌀		
daisies	❁	❁	❁	❁	❁

_____ tulips

_____ roses

_____ daisies

Marko has more tulips than _____.

Marko has fewer _____ than daisies.

Marko has the same number of

_____ and _____.

How many more?

Students' Ages

| 6-year-olds | 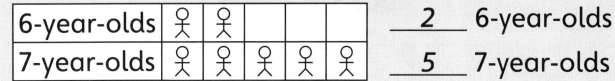 | | | | | _____2_____ 6-year-olds |
| 7-year-olds | | | | | | _____5_____ 7-year-olds |

There are ___3___ more 7-year-olds than 6-year-olds.

Shoes We Have

| Velcro | | | | | | | _____ Velcro |
| laces | | | | | | | _____ laces |

_____ more students have Velcro than laces.

Birds We Saw

| pigeons | | | | | | _____ pigeons |
| robins | | | | | | _____ robins |

We saw _____ more robins than pigeons.

Do We Have Pets?

| have a pet | | | | | | | _____ have a pet. |
| have no pet | | | | | | | _____ have no pet. |

_____ more students have a pet than do not.

☐ Draw ☺ to finish the graph.
How many more or fewer?

Sports We Play

| hockey | ☺ | ☺ | ☺ | | | 3 play hockey. |
| soccer | | | | | | 5 play soccer. |

_____ more students play _____ than _____.

Hand We Write With

| left hand | | | | | | | 2 of us use our left hand. |
| right hand | | | | | | | 6 of us use our right hand. |

_____ fewer of us use our _____ hand.

Our Favourite Pets

cats						4 of us like cats.
hamsters						5 like hamsters.
fish						I boy likes fish.
dogs						3 of us like dogs.

_____ more of us like _____ than _____.

Probability and Data Management 1-5

Tally Charts

☐ Write the number or draw the tally.

| | 1 | || | 2 | ||||̶ | 5 | ||||̶ | 6 |

| ||| | | | | 4 | ||||̶ || | | | | 8 |

| ||||̶ ||||̶ | | | ||||̶ |||| | | | | 11 |

| ||||̶ ||||̶ ||| | | | | | 15 |

| ||||̶ ||||̶ ||||̶ |||| | | | | | 17 |

| | 20 | ||||̶ ||||̶ ||||̶ ||||̶ || | |

| | 25 | ||||̶ ||||̶ ||||̶ ||||̶ ||||̶ ||||̶ | |

☐ Tally the number of objects.
☐ Cross the objects out as you count.

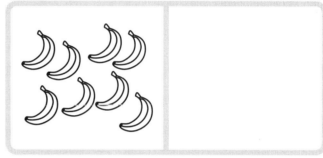

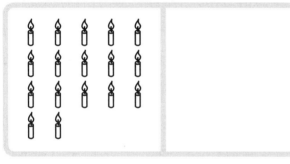

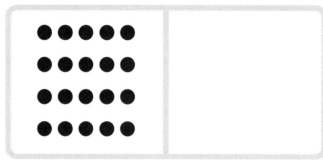

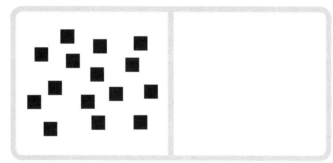

Probability and Data Management 1-6

Ms. C's class had a snack break. Students chose cheese, an apple, or grapes.

Our Snack Today	
cheese	ⅢⅡ
apple	‖
grapes	ⅢⅢⅠ

☐ Answer the questions using the tally chart.

How many students chose **cheese**? _____

How many students chose an **apple**? _____

Did more students choose cheese or an apple?

_____ How many more? _____

What did **the most** students choose for a snack?

_____

What did **the fewest** students choose for a snack?

_____

More About Graphs

☐ Ask a question using the words.

Classes We Attend

gym	😊	😊	😊	😊	😊
art	🎨	🎨			
music	🎵	🎵	🎵		
drama	😎	😎			

how many

How many students attend gym class?

_____

the same number

Which two classes have the same number of students?

the most

What class had the most students?

_____

Hair Colour

blond	🙂	🙂	🙂		
brown	🙂	🙂	🙂	🙂	🙂
red	🙂				
black	🙂	🙂	🙂	🙂	

how many

_____

_____

the most

_____

_____

_____

fewer

_____

_____

_____

☐ Ask a question using the words.
☐ Have a partner answer your questions.

Shapes We Count

how many fewer

How many fewer

circles than triangles

are there?

Answer _____

how many more

_____

_____

_____

Answer _____

Favourite Ice Cream

chocolate	ⵗⵗ ⵗⵗ
vanilla	‖‖
strawberry	ⵗ ‖‖

how many more

_____

_____

_____

Answer _____

the most

_____

_____

_____

Answer _____

Today in gym class, Mr. H is letting the class decide which sport to play.

The Sport We Want to Play

Soccer						
Baseball						
Tennis						

☐ Use the chart to answer the questions.

How many people chose soccer? _____

How many more people chose soccer than baseball? _____

What sport should they play in gym class? Why?

_____

_____

Doing Surveys

Tim's Tally Chart

Tim asked: What animal should be the class mascot?

dog	⊮ |||
cat	⊮
fish	||||
bear	||

What animal was chosen the most?

_____

4 people did not choose any animal.
Tim makes a new row for them.

What would you call the new row? _____

☐ Draw a graph for Tim's data. Use Xs.

Choosing a Mascot for Tim's Class

dog										
cat										
fish										
bear										

Which animal should be the mascot? _____

☐ Choose something you like.
☐ Ask 6 other people if they like it too.
☐ Write your results in the tally chart.

Title: Do We Like _____?

yes	
no	

☐ Make a graph. Use ☺.

Title: Do We Like _____?

yes								
no								

☐ Ask a question about your graph.
☐ Answer it.

_____

_____

_____

_____

Probability and Data Management I-8

Always, Sometimes, or Never?

☐ Put a ✓ on events that **always** happen.
☐ Circle ◯ the events that **sometimes** happen.
☐ Put an ✗ through events that **never** happen.

I will ride a T-rex. 	It will get dark tonight. 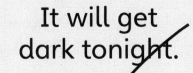 	I will lift an elephant. 
It will snow. 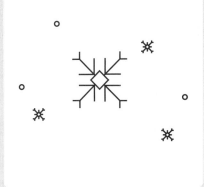	It will rain. 	I will get younger. 
I will be older next year. 	A cow will fly. 	Cookies will grow on trees. 

Certain events **always** happen.

Ed will be older next year.

Impossible events **never** happen.

An alien will study in my class.

☐ Sort the events.

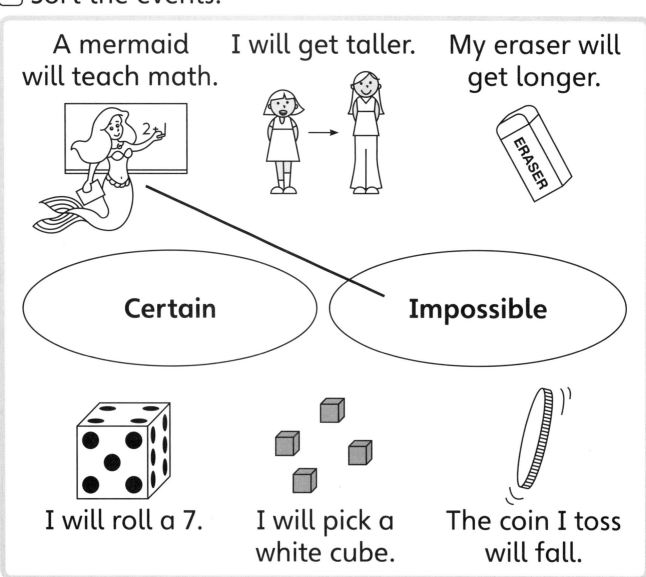

A mermaid will teach math.

I will get taller.

My eraser will get longer.

ERASER

Certain   Impossible

I will roll a 7.

I will pick a white cube.

The coin I toss will fall.

Probability and Data Management 1-9

How Likely?

Some events happen **often**, but not always.

I go to school in the morning.

Some events happen **not so often**.

I will have ice cream for breakfast.

☐ Circle the correct words.

I will eat lunch.

(often)
not so often

It will snow in May.

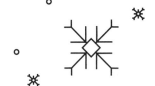

often
not so often

I will win the school raffle.

often
not so often

There will be lightning today.

often
not so often

It will rain in April.

often
not so often

I will go outside for recess.

often
not so often

Likely events happen often, but not always.	**Unlikely** events can happen, but not so often.
 I will go outside tomorrow.	I will lose a tooth tomorrow.

☐ Sort the events.

I will eat a bug today.	I will eat cake for lunch.	It will rain in June.

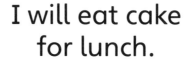

(**Likely**) (**Unlikely**)

It will snow in June.	The sun will shine during a rainstorm.	I will see a car today.

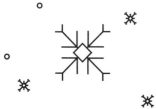  

Probability and Data Management 1-10

☐ Use the best word to describe the event.

| impossible | unlikely | likely | certain |

I will brush
my teeth in the
morning.

_____

I will be
in Grade 2
next year.

_____

I will
lose a tooth
this week.

_____

A pink tiger
will come
to school.

_____

I will have a
birthday
every year.

_____

The next
apple I eat
will be green.

_____

It will get
dark tonight.

_____

I will win the
contest.

_____

I will have a
pet unicorn.

_____

More likely or less likely?

impossible	unlikely	likely	certain
never	not so often	often	always

☐ Circle the event that is **more likely.**

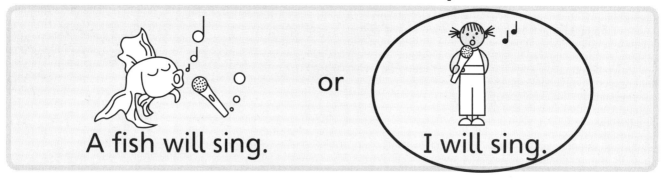

A fish will sing.   or   ⟨ I will sing. ⟩

   or

An ant will have antennae.   A dog will have antennae.

   or

I will be warm.   I will be warm.

   or

It will rain in May.   It will snow in May.

Probability and Data Management 1-10